THE

CODEX

OF

LOVE

revelation from the

White Dove

Second Edition
2009

Ishtar Publishing

Library and Archives Canada Cataloguing in Publication:
Codex of love: Holy Book of World's Oldest Divinity
Released By: Temple of Ishtar
Preface by John Wisdom Gonce III

ISBN 0-9735931-1-3 (pbk.)

1. Goddess religion.
2. Spiritual life.

BL473.5.C64 2005   201'.43
C2005-905170-1

Book Design: Mamdouh Al-Daye
Cover Designer and Artwork: Athena Amato

Ishtar Publishing
141-6200 McKay Avenue,
Suite 716,
Burnaby, BC
Canada V5H-4M9
www.ishtarpublishing.com

TABLE OF CONTENTS

INTRODUCTION TO THE CODEX OF LOVE
by Rev. John Wisdom Gonce, III

Whoever undertakes to set himself up as a judge of Truth and
Knowledge is shipwrecked by the laughter of the gods.

- Albert Einstein

What makes humility so desirable is the marvelous thing it
does to us; it creates in us a capacity for the closest possible
intimacy with God.

- Monica Baldwin

QUANDARY OF A THEOLOGIAN

How do you write an introduction to the Torah, the Quran,
the Upanishads, the Bhagavad-Gita, or the New Testament? If
these ancient scriptures were indeed divinely inspired, how can
any mortal - even one who is considered a "holy man" or "holy
woman," in some sense - have the right to comment on them?
And I know that the Codex of Love is such a book, divinely
inspired and supernaturally revealed.

How would such an introduction - and the book itself - be
received in the skeptical postmodern marketplace of fiercely
competing ideas? When at least two of the world's leading
traditional religions are daily discredited by association with
war and terrorism, how can people help but feel skeptical about
the moral value, if not the legitimacy, of any religious text, when
supposed representatives of "religions of love" suicide-bomb
mosques and synagogues and carpet bomb cities full of women
and children?

The scriptures of the religions they claim to represent cannot
help but come under cynical scrutiny. For we live in a time
not only of skepticism, but of bitter cynicism, when both new
and traditional ideas and ideals, including spiritual values, are
being questioned as never before. Currently, the most respected
pundits of postmodern spirituality, like Ken Wilbur, originator

of the Integral Theory, have been careful to wrap themselves in a cloak of (at least) moderate skepticism. For example, when commenting on childhood spirituality, Wilbur observes:

> Still, in this age of rampant narcissism, the dangers of elevating prerational impulses to transrational liberation far outweigh any skepticism about the glory of the two-year-old child, and although what we ideally want is a judicious assessment of each, erring on the side of skepticism is often the wiser move. [1]

I myself have poured more than a little gasoline on this bonfire of skepticism, and some would say that I have built a literary reputation on the skeptical approach to occultism, metaphysics, and religion. Some have called my book *The Necronomicon Files* "investigative journalism" (among less flattering names), and claimed that it represents a *new genre* of textual criticism and deconstruction (not to mention *debunking*) in occult literature.[2] And I must confess that I was none too gentle in the way I exposed the worst occult hoax of the 20th century. But, as Virginia Postrel once said in defense of Camille Paglia; "The public is sick of pious discourse."

So now, I, the avid Fortean skeptic, the obnoxiously iconoclastic critic, must comment on a *divinely revealed book* that frustrates my native skepticism with its apparent absolute genuineness. What kind of miracle is this, by which a hardened skeptic becomes a true believer? It can only be a miracle of the Goddess!

Perhaps, in the end, you can only write a commentary on a book like the *Codex of Love* in the same spirit as that with which you walk your spiritual path – by faith. So it is by faith, and with a bit of humility, that I write these words, trusting that they will please the Great Goddess Ishtar, who revealed this book.

And yet, even though faith is supposed to be "the substance of things hoped for, the evidence of things not seen." (Hebrews 11:1), faith can also be based (at least partially) on evidence found in the physical world. My faith in the *Codex* is largely based on the amazing parallels between it and the ancient hymns and stories (dare I say *scriptures?*) written about the ancient Goddess Ishtar, from whom the *Codex* was received. These ancient records of Ishtar have been found among the multitude of clay tablets excavated by generations of archeologists working in Iraq and other parts of the Near East, and translated and interpreted by Assyriologists from the late nineteenth century to the present day. I will be illustrating a few of these parallels as you read on. Like many biblical scholars, I will rely on textual criticism and historical literary parallels to prove my points.

However, before we proceed with that, perhaps we should discuss the Goddess Ishtar Herself. And we might be wise to start that discussion by weeding out some common misconceptions about Her.

MYTH-CONCEPTIONS ABOUT THE GREAT GODDESS

> Ignorance is not bliss – it is oblivion.
>
> – Philip Wylie

Many people who have read shoddily written, poorly researched works on mythology imagine that they understand Ishtar, the Great Goddess, and Her nature. In most cases, they couldn't be more wrong! One of the most popular misconceptions is that Ishtar was a cruel and destructive Goddess who delighted in treacherously betraying those who trusted in Her. This notion was spread among the public by the authors of a few common works on mythology, whose research was based on an equally common (and commonly misunderstood) Mesopotamian epic. These authors of generalized works on mythology, marketed to the masses, based their understanding of the Goddess on superficial (mis)interpretations of that most accessible of all ancient Mesopotamian texts – the *Epic of Gilgamesh* – in order to give us a warped understanding of the theology of the ancient Mesopotamians. A prime example of this kind of pseudo-scholarly atrocity can be found in an essay by Felix Guirand:

> ...woe to him whom Ishtar had honoured! The fickle goddess treated her passing lovers cruelly, and the unhappy wretches usually paid dearly for the favours heaped on them. Animals, enslaved by love, lost their native vigour: they fell into traps laid by men or were domesticated by them. 'Thou has loved the lion, mighty in strength', says the hero Gilgamesh to Ishtar,

'and thou hast dug for him seven and seven pits! Thou hast loved the steed, proud in battle, and destined him for the halter, the goad and the whip.'...Even for the gods Ishtar's love was fatal. In her youth the goddess had loved Tammuz, god of the harvest, and – if one is to believe Gilgamesh – this love caused the death of Tammuz.[3]

However, one would be wise *not* to believe Gilgamesh – or Guirand either! In fact, the passage Guirand quoted from the *Epic of Gilgamesh* was nothing more than Gilgamesh's stated *opinion* – an opinion skewed by youthful ignorance, arrogance and hubris! (Other events in the *Epic* illustrate just how ignorant and arrogant Gilgamesh really was at this stage of his life.) Those words were spoken by the *immature Gilgamesh,* before he set out on his quest for immortality or enlightenment and returned a slightly sadder - but much wiser - man. Morever Felix Guirand, who wrote the commentary quoted above, was no Assyriologist; he was, in fact, a kind of mythographer slash journalist. Guirand's works were often disappointing because of his sweeping generalizations and his often superficial understanding of the material about which he wrote.Unfortunately, there have been many "scholars" who were too lazy to look any further than the easily accessible *Epic of Gilgamesh* and were, even then, too simple-minded to give that slap-dash "research" anything but a superficial interpretation.

If Ishtar had truly been the fickle, unreliable, treacherous Goddess of Gilgamesh's diatribe, and if Her favor really led to certain destruction, the bulk of the ancients would probably have declared Her a *demon* and refused to call upon Her. Certainly a people as ruthlessly practical as the ancient Mesopotamians would never have prayed to Her for success, prosperity, good luck, and love as consistently as they did for thousands of years. She would certainly never have been the most popular Goddess in every phase of ancient Mesopotamian history - as indeed she was! According to Jeremy Black and Anthony Green:

The goddess Inana or Ištar was the most important female deity of ancient Mesopotamia at all periods.[4]

Far from being capricious and unreliable, various ancient texts reveal a very different picture of Ishtar. According to them, the love and blessings of Ishtar were as reliable as the sunrise and as solid as the Rock of Gibraltar. For example, the Hittite king, Hattusilis III, who worshiped Ištar of Nineveh, wrote this about his covenant with Ishtar and Her steadfast loyalty to him:

> But my Lady Ishtar appeared to me in a dream, and in the dream said this to me: "Shall I abandon you to a (hostile) god? Do not fear!" And I was cleared from the (hostile) god. Since the goddess, my Lady, held me by the hand, she never abandoned me to the hostile god, (or) the hostile court, and the weapon of an enemy never overthrew me.[5]

In fact, Ishtar's protection of Her beloved ones was so thoroughly reliable that She sometimes fought their battles for them, and insisted that they trust in Her *completely*, and not even devise a defense strategy. When the Assyrian king Assurbanipal was attacked without warning by his enemies, Ishtar told him that She would handle the situation for him and that he need do nothing but rest in faith:

> "You shall stay here, where your residence is! Eat, drink wine, make merry, and praise my godhead until I go and accomplish that task and make you attain your heart's desire. You shall not make a long face, your feet shall not tremble, and you shall not wipe away sweat in the thick of battle."[6]

Perhaps I should also point out that Hattusilis III and Assurbanipal were genuine historical figures whose lives and careers are verified by archeology and documented in historical records, not semi-mythical characters like Gilgamesh, who, if he really lived, may have had a career far different from the one depicted in the *Epic* that bears his name. At any rate, I think the testimony of real historical personages should carry more weight than that of fictional characters.

Perhaps the most common misconception about Ishtar is the belief that Her religion was little more than a front for *sacred prostitution*, which was understood by biblically-oriented scholars of the 19th century as little more than sexual indulgence with a religious justification. This notion has been overturned by current scholarship. While ritual sex undoubtedly played an important role in the religion of Inanna-Ishtar, it had little or nothing in common with the ordinary sex work commonly called *prostitution* in the modern world. As Johanna Stuckey points out:

> Obviously, most scholars did not distinguish between ritual sex and sexuality for pay (Cooper forthcoming). However, ritual sex would not have been prostitution even if the act produced an offering for a temple (Lambert 1992:136). Rather, it would have been an act of worship.[7]

In this case, Ishtar and Her votaries were the victims of biblical propaganda. The perpetrators of this ancient *smear campaign* were the prophets of the Yahwist cult of the Old Testament, who hated the Ishtar cults of Syro-Mesopotamia, especially those of the Assyrians, the Babylonians, and the Canaanites. So the Yahwists did what all political demagogues do - they *lied!* They slandered Ishtar's priestesses as "harlots" and falsely condemned all sexual rituals as "whoredoms." This is the same kind of political doubletalk that sent the U.S. Armed Forces to invade Iraq looking for *weapons of mass destruction*, only to find a few obsolete Soviet scud missiles and small arms.

Stuckey explains how the Yawhist cult played a deceptive game of verbal bait-and-switch as follows:

> In the Hebrew Bible, the word normally translated "sacred or cult prostitute" is qedeshah/qedeshot (feminine singular/plural) and qadesh/qedeshim (masculine singular/plural). These four titles do not occur very often in the Hebrew Bible (Henshaw 1994:218-221).The root qdsh means "set apart, consecrated" (Brown, Driver, and Briggs 1978 (1953):871-874). For the most part, the terms occur in books from Deuteronomy through to II Kings, the so-called Deuteronomistic History, which is especially nationalistic, polemical, and denunciatory of Canaanite religion (Oden 2000:131,132; Olyan 1988:3). The assumption that "sacred prostitution" had not only occurred, but had happened in the context of fertility cults, resulted from the Hebrew Bible's "deliberate" association of qedeshah, "sacred/consecrated woman," with zonah, "prostitute" (Bird 1989:76).[8]

Now that we have addressed some of the major misconceptions about Ishtar, let us examine Her as She really is, and discuss Her role in ancient history (and perhaps even *prehistory*) and theology.

ISHTAR UNVEILED

> Love is the only reality, and it is not mere sentiment. It is the ultimate truth that lies at the heart of creation.
>
> — Rabindranath Tagore

Ishtar (also known as Inanna) is perhaps the oldest Goddess – indeed the oldest *deity* – ever worshiped by humanity. She was worshiped in ancient Sumer, the world's first civilization, which existed in Mesopotamia, in what is now known as Iraq. As the great Sumerologist Samuel Noah Kramer said; "history begins at Sumer." However, there is also ample evidence to show that She was known to the preliterate cultures of the prehistoric Near East.

According to Betty De Shong Meador, who has translated some of the most ancient poetry written about Inanna-Ishtar, there are parallels between Her worship in Sumer, and a much older Goddess religion practiced in the overlapping Neolithic and Chalcolithic cultures that preceded Sumer in Mesopotamia. According to both Meador and archeologist Joan Oates, the Erech-Jamdat Nasr period (3500 to 2900 BCE), the Ubaid Period (5500 to 4000 BCE), the Samarran period (5500 to 4800 BCE), the Halafian period (6000 to 5300 BCE), the Jarmo period (circa 7000 BCE), and even Paleolithic Neanderthal burials (50,000 BCE) found in the Zagros mountains that border Iraq, seem to show evidence for the continuity of the worship of an imminent Goddess. As Meador puts it:

> When in her poetry Enheduanna uses images such as "the first snake" or "mistress eagle," or describes Inanna as a great bird circling the sky, or juxtaposes Inanna's terrible contradictions, we hear echoes of an ancient tradition that reaches back into

the Neolithic.[9]

Quoting similar sources, Professor Johanna Stuckey, noted feminist scholar, and leading authority on Goddess religion and women's spirituality, seems to agree that the religion of Inanna-Ishtar had a prehistoric lineage:

> Inanna's symbols appear on some of the earliest Mesopotamian seals (Adams 1966:12), and she is the first goddess about whom we have written records (Hallo & Van Dijk 1968). However, it is clear that she did not spring into existence with the invention of writing. Throughout Mesopotamia, archaeologists have found a large number of female figurines, dating from as early as the sixth millennium BCE. Some, which may be forerunners of Inanna, display prominent breasts and have their hands under or cupping them, a gesture employed by many later goddesses, among them Inanna. In *Symbols of Prehistoric Mesopotamia*, Beatrice L. Goff traced Mesopotamian symbols from Neolithic times into the historical period. From her study of various symbols and figurines, she concluded that the main concern of the early Mesopotamians was fertility (1963: 21), later one of Inanna's special interests.[10]

Later, in historical times, Inanna was the most important of all Sumerian Goddesses. She had three primary aspects: (1) Goddess of love - including sexual love - and fertility, (2) Goddess of warfare, (3) and Goddess of the planet Venus. Additionally, She had many other rulerships. To cite only a few examples: Her realms of power included weather and rain, and She was often depicted as a storm-Goddess. She was also a Goddess Of justice, who showed mercy to the honest, but harshness to deceivers and evil-doers. Inanna-Ishtar was also associated with dancing: According to Near Eastern tradition, the ancient style of dance we know today as belly dancing (Oriental Dance, or *La Danse du Ventre*) is said to have begun in Her temples.[11]

viii

Inanna's alternative Sumerian names included *Innin, Ennin, Ninnin, Ninni, Ninanna, Ninnar, Innina, Ennina, Irnina, Innini, Nana* and *Nin*, commonly derived from an earlier *Nin-ana* "lady of the heavens", although Gelb (1960) theorized that the oldest form was "Innin" (INNIN) and that *Ninni*, *Nin-anna* and *Irnina* were originally independent Goddesses. Her Akaddian (Semitic) name is Ishtar. That "Inanna" and "Ishtar" are merely alternate names for the same Goddess is indisputably proven by ancient cuneiform texts that use both names interchangeably.

Hymns and stories written in praise of Inanna-Ishtar are perhaps the first real literature in human history. One of the most notable of these was *The Descent of Inanna [to the Underworld]*, which records Ishtar-Inanna's death in the underworld and Her resurrection and return after three days. Written thousands of years before Christ, this account makes Ishtar the first dying and resurrected savior deity in religious history. According to Professor Simo Parpola, the religion of Ishtar was the precursor of Christianity and all other redemptive religions:

> ...the ecstatic cult of Ištar, which in its essence can be defined as an esoteric mystery cult promising its devotees transcendental salvation and eternal life...3. The cornerstone of the cult's doctrine of salvation was the myth of Ištar's descent into the netherworld, in which the goddess plays the role of the Neoplatonic Cosmic Soul. [12]

Enheduanna, who we mentioned briefly, was a daughter of Sargon the Great, the world's first empire-builder, who appointed her High Priestess of the Moon God in the city of Ur. But Enheduanna's personal deity was Inanna, for whom she wrote three magnificent hymns of praise. It is for these three wonderful poems about Inanna that Enheduanna is remembered as the first author in history whose name we know.

Enheduanna referred to her patron Goddess Inanna as NIN-ME-ŠÁ-RA, "the Lady of Many Offices," which infers that She could do many things - or perhaps everything! In fact, other ancient texts depicted Ishtar as the Goddess who reconciled all opposites: She was said to kindle fires and extinguish them, to sow discord and create harmony, to cause disease and bring healing. If Inanna-Ishtar's power ran the full gamut of human experience, and encompassed every principal in the universe, together with its opposite, – the sum total of Yin and Yang – then Her powers must be limitless indeed. In his book *The Treasures of Darkness*, the great Assyriologist Thorkild Jacobsen listed the major Gods of the ancient Mesopotamian pantheon, sketched out their major myths, and defined their duties. Most of them were easily categorized; Enki = Cunning, Utu = Righteousness, and so forth, except for Inanna! When confronted with Her multifaceted personality and multiple rulerships, the only definition Jacobsen could think of for Inanna–Ishtar was "Infinite Variety."[13]

The implications of this are profound. In trying to comprehend Ishtar's seemingly contradictory nature and infinite powers, the ancient Mesopotamians were struggling with theological concepts that were new to the human race: *omniscience*, *omnipresence*, and *omnipotence*. Was Ishtar the first omnipotent, omnipresent deity in religious history? If so, this would explain why Her religion transcended national boundaries. Ištar of Nineveh, for example, was an "international deity" worshiped throughout the Ancient Near East, well beyond the borders of Mesopotamia. It also explains Her persistence in the Mesopotamian pantheon. Gods would come and go throughout Mesopotamian history, as the political regimes that supported them rose and fell, but Ishtar was worshiped in every time and place.

As the great sage Rabindranath Tagore said; "Love is the only reality, and it is not mere sentiment. It is the ultimate truth that lies at the heart of creation." Perhaps it was Ishtar's role as the Goddess of love in all its forms that distinguished Her as an omnipotent and omnipresent deity. If Inanna–Ishtar is indeed the first and ultimate Goddess of love, then She must also be 'the ultimate truth that lies at the heart of creation.' It can be no coincidence that the ancients understood Ishtar as both the Goddess of love and the very life–force itself. In *The Descent of Inanna [to the Underworld]*, when Inanna is killed, all reproduction stopped, threatening to extinguish all life on earth.

Was this ultimate truth, that love lies at the heart of all

creation, known to the ancient Mesopotamians who worshiped Inanna–Ishtar? The highly respected mythographer Dudley Young, in his book *Origins of the Sacred*, implies that it was, when he states that the first urban cultures (those same cultures that worshiped Inanna–Ishtar) began the first religion of love:

> The Mesopotamian discovery of love was in fact a *recovery* and an elaboration of the games we used to play in our innocence, before the fall of alpha-shaman scared us half to death. The fact that we returned to love as soon as we could build some decent walls to keep the lions at bay only indicates how much we were longing to get back to our oldest and best kind of madness. The Sumerians, and to a notable extent the ancient Hindus, in the first flush of urban self-confidence – and unmistakably hot climates – actually elaborated something like a religion of love.[14]

Love is the central characteristic of Ishtar; it is Her *baseline* aspect, the *moral compass* by which She directs Her actions. If the *Codex of Love*, the book you are holding in your hands, is Ishtar's voice speaking to us today, it also must be part of this ancient spiritual tradition – this *religion of love*. So let us now examine the uncanny parallels between the verses of the *Codex* and the ancient hymns, texts, and symbols of Ishtar that are known and verified from archeological and historical sources. It is these which prove that the *Codex* is not some New Age fabrication, but part of a continuity of timeless spirituality that stretches back into an incalculably ancient past.

TEXTS AND PARALLELS

> Scriptures, n. The sacred books of our holy religion, as distinguished from the false and profane writings on which all other faiths are based.
> – Ambrose Bierce, *The Devil's Dictionary*

I would say more about the mundane (earthly) origins of the *Codex* if only more was known about them – or if they were more important. However, of those physical origins, there is simply not much to tell. The story, what there is of it, is pretty straightforward: The *Codex* is said to be a message from the

Goddess Ishtar transmitted by an angel known as the "White Dove" to a small group of people who, I have it on good authority, had little or no knowledge of Assyriology or the history and theology of the Ancient Near East. Therefore they could not have *faked* the striking parallels between the *Codex* and certain ancient texts related to Ishtar.

Perhaps it is just as well that we don't know any more than we do about the origins of the *Codex*, just as well that it is not simply one more of the multitude of "channeled" texts of the New Age in which the personality and reputation of the channeler always seems to outshine that of the "divine intelligence" that supposedly sent the message. When we say that Mohammad "wrote the *Quran*," or that Sanjay "dictated the *Bhagavad-Gita*," or that Paul "wrote the Epistles of the *New Testament*," we somehow trivialize these sacred books by pointing at the human side of their origins. We might as well credit Gutenberg's printing press for the creation of the *Bible*, or I could blame this introduction on the word processing program on my computer. As long as these works were inspired by God, it wouldn't matter if they were written down by half-witted pig farmers, and if they were not, it wouldn't matter if they were penned by the greatest human poets who ever lived! If any text is truly divinely inspired, then the human scribe who transmits it must somehow "disappear" behind the message of the text itself. The messenger is not the message! The words on the pages are only important because they are footprints left by the Divine as it walked across the sands of human consciousness. Perhaps, in the final analysis, the earthly origin of any sacred text is unimportant – if it is truly sacred!

Unfortunately, as this an introduction, I have room here to discuss only a few of the more profound and or conspicuous parallels between the *Codex* and the ancient texts related to Ishtar. Here is a brief sampling of my findings:

a) Time and again in the Codex, Ishtar mentions "My lions." This is significant because the lion is the totem animal most often associated with Her. From the Akkadian Period, the lion is consistently attributed to Ishtar. The Assyrian king Assurbanipal II (reigned 883-859 BCE) dedicated two monumental stone lions to an aspect of Ishtar and set them up at Her temple at Kalhu (modern Nimrud). Additionally, it is almost certainly Ishtar who is depicted standing on a lion on the seventh-century BCE rock panels of Maltai. On the same panels, Mulissu (another aspect of Ishtar) is also shown enthroned on a lion.[15]

b) The Codex repeatedly mentions prophets and prophecy, and even features some apparent prophecies of its own. In one verse, for example, the Goddess states:

> "I have made My blood to run in the veins of saints and prophets and My symbols adorn every faith. I am the hidden flame in every religion and to Me all of you shall return."

This is extremely significant because current scholars believe that, especially in ancient Assyria, Ishtar was a Goddess of prophecy, and prophecy was an integral part of Her religion. As Simo Parpola observes:

> The close connection of Assyrian prophecy to the cult of Ištar has been noted in several earlier studies, and indeed cannot be stressed enough. This close connection is evident not only from the fact that the Assyrian oracles are called words of Ištar/ Mullissu; as shown in detail below (p. IL ff), the prophets also bear names associated with the Goddess or her cult, and come from three major cult centres of Ištar, viz. Arbela, Calah and Assur (the "Inner City"). One of the prophets is a votaress donated to the Goddess by the king. The oracles contain references to the cult of the Goddess or present demands on her behalf.[16]

c) One of the most important of these parallels relates to compassion. Some scholars have tried to dismiss Ishtar as merely a Goddess of sexuality, and argued that this is the only type of "love" She represents. However, many of the ancient hymns and texts tell a very different story. One ancient Akkadian hymn to Ishtar firmly establishes Her as a Goddess of compassion: "She dwells in, she pays heed to, compassion and friendliness."[17] The theological implications of this passage – that the Goddess dwells in compassion – are echoed in the Codex as the Goddess repeatedly proclaims a message of compassion – even tenderness – from its pages.

d) The mystical significance of numbers – and the very *rhythms of language* – found in the *Codex* also mirror those of ancient Mesopotamia. Consider this passage from the sixth verse of the Codex:

> "Seven are the petals of love. Seven are the ways of the heart. Seven are the principles of passion. Seven are the rules of intimacy. Seven are the truths of ecstasy."

Now compare that passage to the one below, translated from an ancient Sumerian magical text:

> "They are the Seven, they are the Seven, they are the Seven from the source of the Apsu, they are Seven, adorned ones in Heaven, who grew up in the source of the Apsu, in the cella."[18]

Now, the passage I just quoted from the *Codex* refers to seven divine principles of love, and the passage quoted directly above, from an ancient Sumerian text, refers to seven demons, but what I am pointing out here is the similarity of *structure*, *style*, and *cosmology* – and even *linguistic rhythms* – found in both texts. Even more significantly, the *repetition of the number seven* occurs in both. In ancient Mesopotamian religion and magic, seven was the number of perfection and completion. According to Jeremy Black and Anthony Green:

> By far the most significant number for the ancient Mesopotamians was seven...In magic, incantations must often be repeated seven times, seven demons expelled, seven gods invoked, ritual actions are carried out seven (or seven times seven) times, seven cylinder seals are hung around the neck of a patient, and so on.[19]

e) Last, but most certainly not least, I am going to mention what I consider one of the most important parallels between the *Codex* and the ancient scriptures of Ishtar. Throughout the *Codex*, the Goddess speaks directly to women, and frequently emphasizes that women are to be treated by their lovers with respect, love, pure passion (as opposed to simple lust), and absolute tenderness. This seems to relate directly to Ishtar's ancient Assyrian epithet; "Lady of Ladies," and to an Akkadian Hymn that emphasizes Her role as the special protector of all women:

> Be it slave, unattached girl, or mother, she preserves (her). One calls on her; among women one names her name.[20]

Hopefully, these few examples will make it obvious as to why I am impressed with the *antiquity* behind this modern book, and why I believe it is the voice of the Goddess - and not some New Age channeler - that speaks to us from its pages. Now that I have examined the ancient aspects of the *Codex*, I would like to comment on its significance for us in the present - and the future.

HER RELIGION OF LOVE

> "My heart has become capable of every form: It is a pasture for gazelles and a monastery for Christian monks, and a temple for idols, and the pilgrim's Ka'ba, and the tablets of the Torah, and the Book of the Koran. I follow the religion of Love; whatever way love's camel takes, that is my religion, my faith."

> - Ibn Arabi (1165-1240),
> Moorish/Spanish Sufi philosopher

Like Ibn Arabi, I have become convinced that religion must not merely *preach* a message of love, but must actually *be* love! Otherwise, it is worthless. For I have also concluded that love is the basis of all life, the source of creation, the very force of attraction that holds atoms and molecules together, the gravitation that keeps stars and planets in rotation, the energetic force that holds together the very cells in my hands as I type these words. I am also convinced that Ishtar is both Love and the life-force that holds all things together. As Dattatreya Siva Baba has said; "Abandoning Vasi is abandoning God." (*Vasi* is the inner prana, the life force.)

Since I have followed Ishtar for over a decade now, and especially since I have read and meditated on certain passages from the *Codex of Love*, I have begun to see that love and (authentic) religion have more than a few things in common. Far greater thinkers than I have also seen these similarities. Take, for example, this observation by the great mythographer Dudley Young, whom some have called "the natural successor to Joseph Campbell":

> What is essentially involved in both love and religion is the repairing of unities broken by experience and beyond that the retrieval of a Unity both all-encompassing and semidiurnal.[21]

The *Codex of Love* is all about repairing unities! It is about repairing the brokenness in women who have been sexually abused. It is about reconciling the conflict between male and female energies that has ravaged modern civilization. It is about restoring the balance between humanity and its environment. Morever, it is about recreating harmony and peace in a civilization subverted by its own fascination with chaos and destruction, and its greed for gain at any cost.

There are many books written about the Goddess, the "old religion," and Neo- Paganism. Experts write from Jungian or anthropological perspectives, and some authors give you a few basic rituals and hymns. The *Codex of Love* stands alone and unique in that it is the living word of the Goddess Herself.

One of the things that impresses me most about the *Codex of Love* is that it is simply not the kind of comfortable "religious book" that a human being would write. It demands too much of us - it demands that we transform! If you read this book, it will change you! If you do not want to change, put this book down now, forget you saw it, and continue in your comfortable rut until it kills you. If you would like to come alive to love, read on, but don't say I didn't warn you!

There is something about reading this book - especially reading it aloud - that rewires the psycho-spiritual circuits of the reader in such a way as to make him or her more susceptible to love in all its forms. This is one of the main reasons I am convinced that it is the voice of Ishtar speaking from the pages of the *Codex*. If the religion of Ishtar stretches back to Neolithic times, then the desire for Ishtar may be hardwired into our DNA. That could explain why She so easily transforms anyone She touches. Ishtar is the Goddess of Transformation! This is how Johanna Stuckey describes the transformational nature of Ishtar:

> All of her various aspects and functions involve transition, boundary crossing, and transformation - food and seed in a storehouse seemingly dead, but alive, poised to become something else; rain which changes infertile to fertile...[22]

I once read a book by a Christian author who claimed that the first impression that comes into your mind is always from your spirit (the so-called "subconscious mind"). We have all had the experience of answering a test question with the first answer that came to mind - and getting it right. If we questioned that intuitive answer and wrote something else, we got it wrong. If the theories of scholars and archeologists like Meador, Stuckey, Oates, and Goff are correct, and the religion of Ishtar stretches back into Neolithic times, and may have been the first religion in history, that means that for some 10,000 years or more, when the universe asked us humans the question: "Who is God?" our immediate answer was: "She is the Great Queen of Heaven and Earth!" Then, a few thousand years ago, we started dithering and doubting that answer - and got it wrong.

For it was about 3,000 years ago that prophetic men from the desert changed the course of religious history on our planet. However, long before the Abrahamic nomads, a living prophetic tradition of women preached the much older religion of the Goddess of love and life itself.

Why should something that happened thousands of years ago matter to you today? It matters because the Goddess' prophetic tradition still lives! Just as *debar Yahweh* (the word of Yahweh) was heard 3000 years ago, the *abat Ishtar* (the word of Ishtar) still cries for you to hear today. It matters because you live in a world poised on the brink of drastic, catastrophic change. It matters because those changes are coming whether you have any spiritual light to guide you through them or not. Last, it matters because the fundamental spiritual and cultural answers that have been in vogue since the late Roman Empire have finally proven themselves worthless – have, in fact, proven themselves the cause of many of our problems.

Everyone feels the quiet before storm. Christians await the second coming of Christ, Muslims the arrival of the Madhi, Jews the Messiah, and Buddhists the bodhisattva Mattreya. Even New Agers await an Ascension which, at the time of this writing is expected to occur in 2012. They may all be right or, more likely, all wrong. Just by the energy of expectation, however, they may cause something (probably unpleasant) to occur.

If Inanna–Ishtar was here with us in preliterate, prehistoric times, and She was with us at the first dawning of human culture, perhaps She was the first light we saw when we emerged from the long, dark night of prehistory. Now, for some reason, She has returned to us in what may very well be our darkest hour.

I believe that She has come back to guide us home – to a home we have never really known before, a true Eden, greater than either the *edin* of the Sumerians or the blighted garden of Genesis. It is garden with no serpentine traps, no forbidden trees, and no sword–wielding archangels, an Eden where the fruits of knowledge and eternal life are freely available to all, and where the divine light of Her love shines throughout eternity.

JOHN WISDOM GONCE III has had a life-long fascination with religion, supernormal phenomena, history, and the occult. As an ordained minister in a Charismatic/Pentecostal denomination, he served as assistant pastor to a small mission church for several years. Now, as a Neo-Pagan and a practicing occultist, he occasionally provides exit counseling for victims of destructive cults. As a student of both fantasy fiction and cinema, John has studied the relationship between film, fiction and the occult for over ten years.

Notes:

[1] "Introduction to the Second Volume of *The Collected Works of Ken Wilber.*" Shambhala Publications, found at *Ken Wilbur Online,* http://

wilber.shambhala.com/html/books/cowokev2_intro.cfm/

[2] "An Interview with Daniel Harms and John Gonce authors of *The Necronomicon Files: The Truth Behind the Legend*" in the magazine *Paranoia, The conspiracy and Paranormal Reader*. Found at http://www.paranoiamagazine.com/necronomicon.html

[3] F. Guirand, entry for "Assyro-Babylonian Mythology" found in: *The New Larousse Encyclopedia of Mythology* (trans. Aldington and Ames), London: Hamlyn, 1968, pp. 49-72.

[4] Jeremy A. Black, Anthony Green, and Tessa Rickards (illustrator) *Gods, Demons and Symbols of Ancient Mesopotamia: An Illustrated Dictionary*. University of Texas Press, Austin, TX, 1992, 2003, page 108.

[5] From "The Apology of Hattusilis III" found in Cyrus H. Gordon's *Forgotten Scripts*, New York, Barnes and Noble. 1993, page 204.

[6] From Assurbanipal Cylinder B, found in Simo Parpola's *Assyrian Prophecies*. Volume IX , Neo-Assyrian Text Corpus Project, Helsinki, Finland. Helsinki University Press, 1997. page XLVII

[7] Johanna H. Stuckey "Sacred Prostitutes" *MatriFocus: Cross-Quarterly for the Goddess Woman*, Samhain 2005, volume 5-1, found at http://www.matrifocus.com/SAM05/spotlight.htm

[8] Johanna H. Stuckey "Sacred Prostitutes" *MatriFocus: Cross-Quarterly for the Goddess Woman*, Samhain 2005, volume 5-1, found at http://www.matrifocus.com/SAM05/spotlight.htm

[9] Betty De Shong Meador, *Inanna, Lady of Largest Heart, Poems of the Sumerian High Priestess Enheduanna*, Austin, TX, University of Texas Press, 2000, page 29.

[10] Johanna H. Stuckey "Inanna, Goddess of 'Infinite Variety,'" *MatriFocus: Cross-Quarterly for the Goddess Woman*, Samhain 2004, volume 4-1, found at http://www.matrifocus.com/SAM04/spotlight.htm

[11] Fatema Mernissi, *Scheherazade Goes West*, New York, NY, Washington Square Press, 2001, page 70.

[12] Simo Parpola, *Assyrian Prophecies*. Volume IX , Neo-Assyrian Text Corpus Project, Helsinki, Finland. Helsinki University Press, 1997. page XV.

[13] Thorkild Jacobsen, *The Treasures of Darkness: A History of Mesopotamian*

Religion, Newhaven and London, Yale University Press, 1976, p. 143.

[14] Dudley Young. *Origins of the Sacred : The Ecstasies of Love and War*, New York, NY, St. Martin's Press, 1991, pp. 159-160.

[15] Jeremy A. Black, Anthony Green, and Tessa Rickards (illustrator) *Gods, Demons and Symbols of Ancient Mesopotamia: An Illustrated Dictionary*. University of Texas Press, Austin, TX, 1992, 2003, page 119.

[16] Simo Parpola, *Assyrian Prophecies*. Volume IX , Neo-Assyrian Text Corpus Project, Helsinki, Finland. Helsinki University Press, 1997. page XLVIII.

[17] "Akkadian Hymn to Ishtar" (circa 1600 BCE) Translated by Ferris J. Stephens, found in: *Religions of the Ancient Near East: Sumero-Akkadian Religious Texts and Ugaritic Epics*, Isaac Mendelssohn (editor). Liberal Arts Press, New York, 1955, page 153.

[18] Exorcistic incantation. Translated by M.J. Geller: *Forerunners to Udug-hul, Sumerian Exorcistic Incantations*. Wiesbaden: Steiner Verlag, 1985 pp 42-3 (lines 401-9) as quoted by the translator in "Freud, magic and Mesopotamia: How the Magic Works" by M.J. Geller, found at: http://findarticles.com/p/articles/mi_m2386/is_v108/ai_20438229/pg_1?tag=artBody;col1

[19] Jeremy A. Black, Anthony Green, and Tessa Rickards (illustrator) *Gods, Demons and Symbols of Ancient Mesopotamia: An Illustrated Dictionary*. University of Texas Press, Austin, TX, 1992, 2003, page 144.
[20] "Akkadian Hymn to Ishtar" (circa 1600 BCE) Translated by Ferris J. Stephens, found in: *Religions of the Ancient Near East: Sumero-Akkadian Religious Texts and Ugaritic Epics*, Isaac Mendelssohn (editor). Liberal Arts Press, New York, 1955, page 153.

[21] Dudley Young. *Origins of the Sacred : The Ecstasies of Love and War*, New York, NY, St. Martin's Press, 1991.

[22] Johanna H. Stuckey "Inanna, Goddess of 'Infinite Variety,'" *MatriFocus: Cross-Quarterly for the Goddess Woman*, Samhain 2004, volume 4-1, found at http://www.matrifocus.com/SAM04/spotlight.htm

White Dove

O seeker of love and passion, live, for they are life; laugh, for they are joy; cry, for in them is pain of truth. ⚶

Seek not the embrace of a lover, but of love; seek not to be loved once, but to love always. ♀

White Dove

Silence! Silence! Silence! Listen to the beat of love, for in the heart is truth, and in silence is wisdom and understanding. ♀

The greatest wisdom you can teach a young woman is how to choose her man. ♀

White Dove

*T*here is the lover in her dream, the lover in her life, a mate, and a friend. Unless she chooses wisely, her dreams will be shattered, her heart broken, and sorrow and loneliness will descend. ♀

t is best if she can turn her friend into a mate, turn her mate into her lover, and merge her lover with the man in her dreams. This is the secret of marriage, and the hidden violets of life. ♀

White Dove

Seven are the petals of love. Seven are the ways of the heart. Seven are the principles of passion. Seven are the methods of intimacy. Seven are the truths of ecstasy. Seven are the pains of rapture. One is the embrace of Light. Who knows of them, knows the forty-nine petalled rose of Life, and the seven visions of God. ✟

ittle can I say of this rose, for it rests in your heart. Seek out My star for it is the stem of the rose. ⚥

White Dove

When your mind is open to My star, your heart to love and your genitals to the triangle of passion, bringing all together in the center, form the name of whom you seek to be touched by your love and passion. ☥

Codex of Love

A woman who shuns the love of men, may uphold her honor, but she fills her cup with sorrow. A man that seeks a woman without love may fulfill his desire, but he will fill his cup with loneliness. These are the laws of love; know them well. ♀

White Dove

$\mathcal{T}$o her who seeks My voice upon rising, sing My name the number of petals in My rose. Then chant, "Mara Mara Ishtar Mara," while rubbing your womb thrice. ♀

𝒜rouse thyself and before the expansion, call upon My lions and ride into the dreams of thine lover. ♀

12

White Dove

If a man seeks a lover, let him light a candle in My name, and burn rosemary as the scent. Let him also gather seven stones and speak over them the ways of the heart: truth, fidelity, compassion, sacrifice, nakedness, tenderness and sweetness. Cover My stones with the wax of My candle, and carry them close to the heart. Let their heat be its guiding lantern. Beware lest your mind cloud your decision. For as your stones grow in heat, so will the seed of love in your heart. ♀

If a woman desires a lover, she should gather seven seashells in My name. Under the light of the moon, let her place a raisin in each one. Holding them close to her chest, recite on each of them the seven ways of the heart. Let her carry them close to her heart and wait for the heat. If she questions the sign, let her listen closer in silence. Once she has conquered her fears, let her hand him the raisins to eat. ☥

White Dove

ine lions are ready to jump on she who is afraid of her passions, who places words where touch should be, who places fear where her heart should be, and who speaks lies where her truth should be. For they are the horses of passion and I am their bridle. ♀

It is not the words that you speak that are keys to romance, but it is the intimacy that your heart hides between them. ♀

White Dove

or him that is afraid of giving and love, let him not play with passion. For love is the father and intimacy is the mother of passion. ♀

*I*n the embrace of a lover seek the exchange of breath, the closeness of the heart and stare deep into the eyes. In them are the three keys to the embrace of the soul and the soaring of the heart. ⚥

White Dove

have given the brightness of My crown to the stars. I have given the vision of My eyes to cats and lions. I have cast My spear into the dragon and unleashed passion. I have given the strings of My harp to My daughters and made their voices sweet to the host of heaven. I have placed the feathers of My wings in the scales of judgment to weigh against the dead hearts. I have made My blood to run in the veins of saints and prophets and My symbols adorn every faith. I am the hidden flame in every religion and to Me all of you shall return. ♀

Codex of Love

Ask not what your lover can do for you but what you can do for her. Ask not that his heart be yours for the taking, but fill its emptiness with your love and essence. ⚀

White Dove

She who seeks to know Me knows of love. She that fears Me fears her heart. She that seeks to unite with Me cares not for pride. ☥

Codex of Love

Pride is a cover for the fear of intimacy, for there is nakedness in love that is undesired. ♀

White Dove

If your lover's touch turns cold and your passions are extinguished, hurry not to find another lover. Tend to the memories of your love and let it warm you. Through its heat, you will ignite the torch of passion even brighter. If coldness overtakes you and the memories forsake you, call upon Me and My fires will descend and passion will engulf you. ☦

Codex of Love

$\mathcal{A}$ true lover knows when love ends
and desire for intimacy begins. For it is at
this point that friendship can be developed. ⚕

White Dove

When a woman stops listening to the beat of her own heart, sorrow can enter the house. ☥

Codex of Love

$\mathcal{I}$f you wonder about the heart of your lover, test not his heart by the words of love, but by the intimacy of touch and the acts of closeness. ♀

White Dove

ove, like a sword, must always be kept clean and sharp, lest it be covered with dullness and rust. ♀

*T*wice have I mentioned the ways of the heart, but only once will I mention the principles of passion. Spontaneity, for who calculates their passion extinguishes it. Individuality, for how can you arouse the passions of your lover if your own elude you. Heat, for passion served cold is naught but the venom of spite and malice. Arousal, for passion without arousal is like the sun during its eclipse. Courage, for passion isn't for the weak of heart or hesitant. Liberation, for no soul is trapped when passion is the horse of its chariot. Surrender, for only to the arms of your beloved will passion release you. These are its principles; unleash it. For without passion, prayers are not answered. ☥

White Dove

f a woman finds passion in the arms of a man, she must listen to the beat of his heart lest its fires scourge her. ♀

He who desires love and increase of passion, let him remember that silence is the first step toward unity, and touch is the key to intimacy. ☥

White Dove

What lies in the eyes but the wisdom of eternal love? This wisdom carries the fruits of time. In the fruits are the seeds of faith. These seeds will give fruit to the plants of hope. Hope will shield them from the dark rays of passion. I give My children these plants, so that their shade will ease their pain. ☥

Codex of Love

$\mathcal{S}$he who wields My passion should do so with a pure heart, for impure passion is a serpent unleashing its fury on the children of love. ☥

White Dove

Passion aroused by need is like emptiness leading to emptiness. ☥

Codex of Love

Despise not passion for it is like fire; tend to it and it will warm you; unleash it and it will burn you; extinguish it and it will freeze you. ⚥

White Dove

ime has passed since the ancient temples of love have been erected. Today the world has erected other shrines made of stone. Love has been sold cheap to all bidders. I remind all that love cannot be bought, but exists in the hearts and minds of all that love. Make your room a shrine, let the smell of roses descend as you lie in the arms of ecstasy. Remind yourself that unless you give yourself in love there is no shrine. ☥

When the silence descends between you and a lover, learn to speak with your eyes and hands, lest silence becomes your mate. ⚥

White Dove

Is that truth that your lips utter, O lover? Is that passion that your fingers seek to touch, O lover? Is that ecstasy that arouses your senses, O lover? Is the chalice of intimacy your wine, O lover? Do you know of what I ask? I ask of your heart, does it beat with her name? I ask of your blood, does it carry her breath? I ask of your cheeks, do they know your tears? Blessed art thou, O lover, who knows of these. Thou art the savior of hearts and a fountain of joy. She is your hope and you are her life. This is love, so listen well, O ears, and behold, O eyes, the story of the King and Queen. ☥

Codex of Love

*T*ruth, My children, is not an epic or an enigma. It is not filled with moral seeds or the judgment of minds. It can't be explained by words or measured by numbers. It need not be discovered or realized. Truth is what a lie isn't. Truth rests where peace descends. Truth engulfs a heart embraced by love. I now share with you a truth. Love is real; let it be your faith. ☥

White Dove

ave you asked if there is a God? Have you wondered if love is real? I now answer you and say love is real. God is love. Believe, if you wish; ignore this truth if you may, but end your pain. That is all that God asks of you, to know him, to know love, to know peace. Have hope in that, if you but please. ☩

Codex of Love

*T*he world is deafened by the tears of pain. Children are being born to a world that lost its heart. Is it not enough the soil of the earth has been poisoned with hate? You struggle among you to build towers to reach the sky. We watch and I ask, when will you stop to enjoy paradise? When will the children of this world dance with the stars and play with peace? ♰

White Dove

have sung to you of love. I have whispered to you the fires of passion. I have shared with you the heart of truth. I have pleaded for peace. I have cried for you children, heavenly tears. I ask you now, what miracle do you need to fill your life with love and peace? ☥

*W*ho comes between the lover and the beloved? I am the beloved and you are My love. They say gods, I say God. They say father, I say I am. I am thy father and I am your mother. I am the King and the Queen. I am that I am. I am Yahuah. I am Ishtar. I am the first and I am the last. I am thy breath and thy sigh. I am the tear and the cry. I hear your prayer before your lips utter it. I am love and wrath. I am justice and truth. *Thou shalt have no other gods before Me.*

What words can capture the essence of love? What truth can be portrayed by the stroke of brushes? What life can you capture in a stone? What brilliance is there to a lie?

White Dove

What faith can you put in a shooting star?
Thou shalt not make unto you a graven image.

If the angels poured all the blood shed in the name of Heaven, the sea would be red. If the angels covered the earth with every coin harvested in the name of Heaven, there shall be no sand. If the angels placed every law struck by man in the name of Heaven, My scales would break. If the angels wrote of every evil sowed by man in the name of Heaven, the pen would be dry. Did you all not hear? *Thou shall not take the name of thy God in vain.*

Have you heard of the day of rest? I descend to weigh the hearts of men. I descend to honor the sorrows of women. It is a day your Father honored your Mother. It is a night for a man to please his lover. This is the time angels shed blood to protect your children. Let the day of the star be a day of prayer. Let the noon of sorrow be an

afternoon of peace. Let the eve of the moon be her loving treat. *Keep the Sabbath.*

Your Father sprung forth life. Your Mother sprung forth love. Their union in heaven sprung forth light. Each child born is the seed of this union. You are the gardeners of this seed. Once the seed grows, it will become but another gardener. If you nourish it, it will nourish another. If you desecrate it, it will desecrate another. When you behold the seeds remember the commandment: *Honor thy Father and thy Mother.*

All darkness bows before the flicker of a light. All despair dissolves before the flicker of a hope. All sorrow departs before the flicker of a joy. All loneliness fades before the flicker of love. All doves sing before the flicker of peace. It is only a flicker, *so do not kill.*

When two hearts mate, little room is left for a second, let alone a third. When two bodies

mate, their fire is fuelled by each other's touch. When two minds mate, a third is formed. Marriage is when two souls mate to give birth to another. For heart mates, love will grow as they proclaim it for all to see. For body mates, passion will grow as their skin is touched by the many fingers of innocence. For mind mates, knowledge will grow as the child teaches the parents. Marriage will grow as the souls ascend, mated in heart, body, and mind. *So, commit not adultery.*

A dream is like a shining jewel. A lover is like a brilliant ruby. A faith is like a rare emerald. The blessings of Light are like brilliant stones. Those that hold them are like children. Who are they that rob children of their dreams? *Thou shalt not steal.*

Words of Truth are like fruits with many healthy seeds. Each seed will grow and

carry many fruits. All of you share the same garden. *Thou shalt not bear false witness against thy neighbor.*

In each of you is a shrine. Within the shrine is an altar. On this altar rests faith. With faith comes peace. In peace rises joy. With joy, an increase in passion. Within its fire is ecstasy. Through ecstasy grows faith. This faith is placed in what every heart holds dear. *Do not covet thy neighbor.*

These are the commandments given then and given now. They were given to the poorest nation and are now given to all nations. Truth is truth. Do you feel it, O men of faith? ♀

White Dove

ave I not told you the story of the three roses? There were three roses - a blue, a yellow, and a white. The blue was the mother of all roses. The yellow was her daughter and the white was the infant grandchild. The blue rose turned to the yellow and asked, "My daughter, do you know what truth lies in roses?" The yellow answered, "No mother, teach me, for I am your daughter. From you flows wisdom, and from me there shall be understanding" The blue rose said, "Tell me, O daughter, the name of the infant white rose?" The yellow answered, "Her name is peace". The blue rose asked, "What is my name?" The yellow rose answered, "You are liberty and I am devotion".

The blue rose shed a petal and said, "Take away hope and you take away liberty". The blue rose shed a second petal and said, "Take away her sister faith and you take

away liberty". The blue rose shed a third petal and said, "Take away understanding and you take away liberty". The blue rose shed its fourth petal and said, "Take away her sister clarity and you take away liberty." The blue rose shed its fifth petal and said, "Take away silence and you take away liberty." The blue rose shed its sixth petal and said, "Take away her sister tranquillity and you take away liberty." The blue rose shed its seventh petal and said, "Take away passion and you take away liberty."

The blue rose then said, "As I shed my last petal I remind you, only through your devotion to your child will the red rose give birth to a blue blossom. My children, all roses rest under the bottom of your heart. They blossom when you blossom and wither when your hearts wither. Do you all not yearn for the blue rose?" ⚥

White Dove

ave you heard Truth, O son of man? Have you heard Truth, O child of the land? Have you heard the cry of the crow? It brings you the news of the sad. It flies with Her pain. It carries Her sorrows. Listen to Truth, O man. If you listen, She will smile. She will raise you in Her scales. She will feed you with Her peace. She will bear your child. Do you not care, O son of man, for the mother of your hope and faith? ☥

The blackness in a mirror is like the shadows of a love lost; it blocks you from reflecting on the love you have. ☦

White Dove

A ship on an ocean, traveling the sea and the waves, seeks to bring to safety the fruits and the treasures that it carries. Each of you is a ship. If you lose your cargo your journey will be for naught. In each of you is a dream. That dream must reach the shore. Treasure your dreams, and do not fear the waves of the ocean. ♀

Codex of Love

ove of a man is like the leaf in winter. Love of a woman is like the leaf in summer. In between lies the beginning of hope and despair. Let faith be the fuel of your hope and love the antidote to your despair. The women amongst you are the containers of both. That is why we have placed the Gardens of Heaven under their feet. ☥

White Dove

The waves of the oceans are but the ripples in the pond of Truth. Hearts devoid of truth fear the waves. Hearts assailed with hate drown in the ripples. Hearts filled with the light of Love make the waves and fill the pond with tears of rapture. ♀

y daughters, you have heard the words of the Lord of Heaven. You have seen what deeds men have done in the name of truth. I now cry to you from behind the Gate of Eternal Silence. I throw to you the wand of faith. Lead the nations back to peace. Erect in your hearts the shrine of truth. Make your bodies sacred temples of love. Let your lips be doorways to understanding. Let your feet carry you with compassion. Peace be upon you the day you are born. Peace be upon you the day you know. Peace be upon you the day to us you return. Peace be upon you, O angels of peace. ☥

White Dove

$\mathcal{T}$he gates of heaven stand open before those that know Light. The gate is opened to all those that know love. The gates are open to those that showed mercy to the poor. The gates are open to all children and those that are old. The gates are open to those who value life. The gates are closed to all those who peddle the Law of Heaven. The gates are closed to those whose hearts are cold and mercy is a weakness, compassion is a vice, and love is for fools. Now you know, walk through the gates. ♀

Codex of Love

What is it that gives a woman's skin pleasure? It is the softness in touch and tenderness of flesh. Arouse the heat slowly like a furnace. Let your lips be the tongue of your love, and your tongue the keeper of its passion. ☥

A woman's tongue is her rod of desire. In its embrace ecstasy is created. Let it dance on the skin of its lover. Seek not the genitals until the cries of rapture deafen your ears. ♀

White Dove

The genitals are receivers of the Light only when the mind is open to the star of the crown; otherwise it's a projector of heat and passion. ☥

White Dove

A lover's womb is the furnace of her passions. Awaken its fire when the glory has entered your mind, and love has taken you into his arms. When the furnace has been filled with the seeds of your love, seal it. Let the rod of creation melt in the heat of the furnace. Let the words of love flow, and let breath fill you with ecstasy. When the holy presence departs from your midst, retract the rod in reverence for the beloved. Cool the furnace with a joined swirling touch. ☥

When two genitals embrace, a torch is lit. Love fuels its light and illuminates the darkness of the world. Lust exhausts its heat and extinguishes the seed of its fire. When two genitals embrace in love, angels sing of life; in lust, angels cry for a broken heart. When two genitals embrace in love, the cycle is complete and I descend; in lust a cycle is born, and I watch. When two genitals embrace in love, I behold My King; in lust, I behold the eclipse of a sun. When two genitals embrace in love, the spirit of Light descends; in lust, sorrow and sickness grow. Love is the meaning of marriage. Lust is the idol of prostitution. Many are they who are married in prostitution. Many are they who fornicate for love. When the pure in heart meet, pure Light fills their wedlock. ♰

White Dove

$\mathcal{T}$o be one with passion is to open your heart, genitals, hands and feet, and absorb with the eyes. ⚥

reath is the carrier of the spirit of passion. Let the breath of your beloved fill you with sweetness. Let your breath teach your beloved of its heat. Let the breath embrace the rod and vulva with its life. Learn to liberate your love in the wings of the breath. The breath of pure passion can fill your mind with heat and wonder. My desires are My breath, and from it springs forth all life. ♀

White Dove

*H*ave you heard the cry of the rod? It drives men into the ravine of loneliness. Its sobbing echoes and deafens the ears of love. Have you heard of the wailing of the vulva? Its emptiness drives women into the arms of the night. Its confusion and sorrow cloud the hearts of love. What is it that each seeks? They seek the tenderness of a lover and the understanding of a friend. Each seeks another; let the rejoicing begin. The distance between the hearts of two lovers is the quickness of breath. Open your eyes and let the Light descend. ☥

Codex of Love

*T*o be one with compassion is to know when to speak the words of love. To be one with cruelty is to speak a lie within the rays of passion. ♀

White Dove

*T*reat the woman of your life as a virgin bride. For there is only but one light, that lets her body be filled with sweetness and her heart shine bright. It's the fires of a groom that doesn't grow old, and of his bride forget. Let her be the virgin in your life, and the fire of your light. If her body grows tired, awaken it with sweetness of your touch. If her mind grows afar, remind her of the passion that flames and darts. If she seeks another love, beware, lest your jealousy of the bridge tear apart. A bride and a groom are like water and fire. Too little water, the fire loses its steam. Too much fire, the water evaporates under the raging heat. Too much water, the passion departs and love will grow cold to the touch. Passion is the fire of love and intimacy, the water of marriage. She is the moon and you're the sun. Without each of you, the world will grow dark. ♰

Codex of Love

What is it that you all seek in the glory of the world? I am the Light of Radiance, the Spirit of Life, the Glory of the World. I am the Mother of the Child, and the Child Mother. There is one glory in the world that remains hidden and veiled. It lies under the fingers of the Beloved. O seeker of glory, be a lover. And the Beloved shall touch you with His fingers. O My children, I tell you. The time for love is at hand. Let the Glory descend. Ah! My Soul! It devours the wrath of My Beloved. There shall be peace. ☥

White Dove

isten, O men, to the secrets of tenderness. In passion, give more than you receive. In love, listen before you see. Touch her body as if it is but a flower ready to blossom. Let her be your friend, not just a lover. Treat her as an angel of sweetness and the bird of freedom. Tend to her broken wing and let her fly to the rays of the sun. Be tender and to your arms she will always fly. ♀

Codex of Love

O seeker of truth! Open the gate of heaven. Walk upon the straight and narrow path. Do you know of what I speak? I speak of your heart, its joy and pain. I speak of your life, its glory and despair. I speak of your mind, its wisdom and confusion. I speak of your dream, its boundaries and disillusion. The gate rests with peace and opens with love. It renders open with but a smile of a beloved. The path is narrow, for there can be no hate. It is straight, for it harbors no lie.

She in your arms is the key. In her chest lies a truth. In her tears, she sheds pain. If the truth is pain, how can you ask for the gate to open? His heart, My daughter, is the

White Dove

path on the road. If it wavers in your arms, strengthen it. Take not each for granted. The heart knows and the soul records. A broken heart is a broken promise. The promise is the key. Your dream is the fruit and life is the gate. ♀

Codex of Love

What is it that all tears cry for? They cry for peace and its embrace. They cry for love and its turmoil. They cry for the children of the world. What is it that all angels pray for? They pray for the world to be healed. They pray for the young souls to know. They pray for the pure among you to teach. What is it that is all I ask for? I ask for the children to be healed. I ask for the brides to be loved. I ask for men to know peace. I ask all of you to each other feed. What have we asked that you can't bear? Don't defame the truth, for there is only one way. It begins in your heart and it ends in rapture. ☥

White Dove

$\mathcal{P}$assion is the moving rod of the wheel of life. If it departs, a woman's life is like but a memory. If it exceeds, a woman's life can lose the ropes of safety. Bring your passions to the spirit of love. The wheel will turn and your life will be but a dream. Passion is a root. Plant it in the garden of hope and it will never wither. Plant it in the garden of fear and its leaves on your life will feed. Now you know, so ask Me not for its secrets. It lies in your womb, it grows in your heart and it fruits in your actions. If your passions you have lost, welcome to the tower of lust. ☥

71

Codex of Love

When My children return, back to Me, the torches of peace will shine. For when a child desecrates his own mother, his heart doesn't know peace. If your own mother becomes your enemy, who is your friend? Those that sever the hands that feed them shall die hungry. Those that sever the cords of love shall die lonely. Those that only seek the veneration of their tribe shall be with no honor. Your mother has fed you, it is her you must love and honor. ☥

White Dove

hen you hold your lover in your arms, treasure her; for she is My gift to you. Tend to her pleasures and carry her upon the palms of your soul. Fill her heart with joy, her womb with the fruits of life, and warm her with tenderness. ⚧

Codex of Love

When a woman beholds her lover, she must remember that he is the shepherd that brings home the milk. She must learn to speak to his heart and not his body. For a woman that awakens a man's heart shall never be cold in the winter or thirsty in summer. To a woman, her shepherd may not be her lover and her lover may not be her shepherd. A woman that seeks out both shall lose her shepherd, and a woman that seeks out only a lover shall have both. These are the laws My child, so sow your seeds well. ☥

White Dove

The world is the playground of love;
know its rules and play its game. Worry
not what others may think, for only love
can judge you. It is not how many lovers
you have, but how many lovers you have
tended to. When the flame of love dies,
so does the bond of marriage. Therefore,
those that quit the labors of their hands
are the poor among you. Enrich your spirit
with joy, your heart with love, and your
labors with its cause. ♀

Codex of Love

To create the Elixir of Love, milk the vulva thrice, then gather the elixir. Add to it thrice rose water and a drop of honey; drink it, for this is the wine of enchantment. ♀

White Dove

$\mathcal{M}$ix the Holy Milk with honey,
flour, and eggs, then bring it unto Me, for
this is the bread of enchantment. ☦

*M*any stars are born. Many stars light the way of the heavens. Each star has a story. If you listen you will catch it and it will awaken you. It will remind you of the wisdom of ages, the secret of all the sages. Listen, for no star shines forever. You each are a star. Tell your story and listen. ☥

White Dove

n the heart of Babylon are two women. One is crowned and the other is dethroned. The men of Babel crowned their lust and dethroned their Queen. They lavished in the flesh of My children and ignored their tears. They saluted the nakedness of their brides and chained their mothers. I now say this: I am the Queen, but where are the men of Babel? ☥

*T*he stars uttered a story at the birth of creation. Love was that story. Do you remember counting the stars? They remember your story — the story of a lover and a beloved, the story of a child and an adult. Tell your story to the stars, for they too count the tears and joys of your heart. Treasure the love in your heart, for it is part of the great story. ♀

White Dove

*T*ell Me, O women, of your pain. Cry
to Me your despair. I listen to your sorrows
and wail. Do you remember the stars from
which you came? Do you remember your
heart, My child? In it is the seed of your
power. Men don't know how to water the
tenderness of its leaves. Time, too, will not
attend nor heal. You are the gardener and
the garden. You are the seed and the fruit.
Love is but your child; be its friend. Your
body is your sanctuary; keep it holy. Your
passion is your will, train it wisely. Joy is
your sister, let her comb your hair. Grow
with love and My tears will quench your
thirst, and My blood for you I will shed.
Do you yet not know Me? I am truth and
liberty. ✝

*T*ears that fall from the eyes of children are like the blood of angels. If sorrow and pain engulfs the heart of a child, an angel's wings turn black with pain. Do not kill the children, for it is these feathers that will weigh your hearts before Me. ✝

White Dove

ather the grass of the vulva, burn it under the full face of My father Sin. Let him heal the burning fires of all unwanted lovers. Let it purify your passions and clear away your pain. ⚥

hy, but why, do women fear the embrace of love and the tingling key to their passions? Why, but why, do they hide behind the curtains of their sorrows? Why, but why, do they not walk naked before their love and demand what is theirs should be given? They should embrace love in My name and let their passion bring them closer to understanding My joys and pain. Women have been born with the tools for love and passion and through them, they will know Light. Men have been born with the tools of procreation and with them, they will continue the seed of Life. Why have the roles been reversed and with it fear and helplessness? ♀

White Dove

*T*he words of truth are spoken through the eyes, while your lips join your lover. Learn to read them and you shall not be deceived in love again. The eyes are the doorways to enchantment, and enchantment can fire up your passion. Lovers speak the silent language of pleasure. Let your heart be your tongue and your eyes the lips that utter the words. Ah! My soul yearns for My lover; where is he? Where is My king? ⚥

When invoking passion, arouse the breasts, then the thighs, and the neck. Add heat to the passion by words of love. Hurry not to milk the vulva, for you may quench the passion, or spill the milk. ☥

White Dove

On the vulva there are many secrets hidden; they can only be discovered with stillness and contemplation. Let thine sweet lips create the ecstasy. ♀

Plough the back of the ears, the shadows of the breast, and the secret flower until the sweat of passion fills your entire being. Hurry not, for what farmer is done before the setting sun? ♀

White Dove

On the soul of the world rests a heart. In the heart lays a tear dropped by an angel, a child born from the blood of the first bloodshed. When the river of blood dries, so will this tear. ☥

Behold the rod of life and pain. Used in My name, it's creation. Used in His name, it's life. Used in your name, it's pain. The rod of joy is the rod of love. The rod of life is the rod of intimacy. The rod of creation is the rod of desire. The rod of pain is the rod of lust. Use the rod in My name, for its seed is mine to take. ♱

White Dove

ove is a ray of light sent from the heart of a lover. The ray travels through the winds of time, and seeks to penetrate the heart of the beloved. If the heart absorbs the ray, it ignites its fire and awakens the seed of passion. If it reflects the ray, it weakens and the fires become logic. Reflect not the ray, but transmute its fire. Let it become a flame of light in your lantern to illuminate the soul of the lover. This is the key of mercy and the way to universal love. ☿

*T*here are many truths in ecstasy. Seven are its dimensions. The first truth of ecstasy is understanding divinity. The second truth is understanding humanity. The third truth is understanding time and illusion. The fourth truth is overcoming desire and its delusions. The fifth truth is the principles of unity. The sixth truth of ecstasy is the voice of music. The last truth of ecstasy is ecstasy. In ecstasy is truth. Truth devoid of ecstasy is a lie. ☥

White Dove

The road to Jerusalem is paved with roses. Each rose is dipped with blood, shed in the name of Light. What say ye, O Jerusalem, to the pilgrims of the Holy Land? Can the rivers of wine be turned to blood? Can you erect shrines on hate? Can you pray with fear in your heart? Where is the Truth your Lord has taught? Where are the Laws your Mother has brought? I wear a black veil of sorrow for the injustice you all have caused. The land of Holies has one keeper, crowned with twelve stars and the banner of peace. All who despise Her, O lions do cast out. I am Jerusalem, the land of red peace. ✝

*T*ake away the hatred from your hearts, O men. Depart from sorrow and doubt, O daughters. Walk with peace and love. Arouse your hearts with light and hope. Be a token of mercy and to each other a friend. Cry not for your loss, and quest not for what your hearts despise. The laws of men die with men. The laws of love are born with every heart. If fear be your master, your life will suffer loss. Fear is a chain of despair and a way to grief. In your life there can only be one master, so chose wisely. ✝

White Dove

say to you, My children, what use
are these things you create, if your hearts
remain cold? You ask what happens
at death? I ask what remains at death?
What remains here but the memories of
your beloved, and those whom you have
touched? Now is the time to create them
with your heart. For soon you will re-enter
My womb. ☥

Listen to the heartbeat of your beloved as you slumber and your morning will only grow brighter. ⚲

White Dove

She who learns to sing to her man in his sleep will only shine brighter in his heart. She who knows Me fears not that love will flee. For a woman's fear can weaken her heart and starve her beloved. ♀

ou ask, where can I find love? I answer just love, love, and love. Then get ready to be stripped naked by love, for he shall overtake you in his arms. ♀

White Dove

f you question the words of truth, but ask what truth was in life, what truth can be found in the embrace of your beloved, what truth can be found in the hearts of children? Truth is not in words, but is scribed on the foreheads of children, on the souls of the innocent whose hearts don't lie. Truth holds the key to knowing spirit. Share your truth and let the spirit of Light be your tongue, for it shall carve words that will dazzle the blind that walk among you. Truth is the child of love and the father of knowledge. Seek the knowledge of the greatest truth, which is love. I am Ishtar. ♀

Why do lovers wonder of the nature of love? Do they not know its petals of ecstasy? Love's petals lie in its abundance. They lie in its reception. They lie in its reciprocity. They lie in its union. They lie in its surrender. They lie in its perception. They lie in its expansion. The petals of love are thus counted seven, yet one in motion. Ecstasy is the elixir of the immortal pomegranate. Love is its seeds, passion is its juice and pain is the sourness of its skin. ☥

White Dove

$\mathcal{T}$ruth is a beautiful sword in the hand of a lover. Used, it can sever the chains of despair and the bonds of doubt. Truth and beauty are sisters, one is the blade and the other the handle. Truth is beauty spoken. Beauty is truth perceived. Teach your eyes to perceive true beauty, less they be deceived by a lie. ⚥

ove is the weapon of the meek. Truth is the faith of the blessed. Courage is the garment of the innocent. Such are the words. ♀

White Dove

he dark spear of sorrow seeks out those that desecrate My children and violate My daughters. They are the jewels of love and seeds of light. Crown thy women, for in them is the power to raise a nation. Shield thy children, for in them are the seeds of generations. O, My sons, listen to the truth they bring you and honor thy covenant. ☦

*T*ruth devoid of hope is the torch of illusion. Reality concealed in a lie is the sad story of life. A lover entwined in his love is the garment of illumination. I am the declaration of this truth to you. I reside in the illumination of hope. Eternal salvation is but the quickness of breath in pursuit of rapture. Love has filled the souls of the blessed. Learn of this love, for your world is losing the torch of hope. ♀

White Dove

Hear Me O My daughter, for I call you with every sigh. I seek you when you cry. I bring you the medicine to the pain in your heart. Do not shun Me, for I am your mother. ☥

ight, love, and truth are the bases of passion. Passion is the ruler of the wilderness; the wilderness is when the soul yearns for unity. ♀

White Dove

etween the Sun and the Moon rests the shrine of time. This shrine holds a key, gold and bright. This key is adorned with three jewels and a cross. The jewels are blue, red, and yellow and the cross is white. When the Sun conjoins the Moon, the shrine opens. The key can seal the dragon in slumber till another void moon. To seal the dragon, spin the wheel of life or a partner choose. Before they conjoin, awaken the Star of the East. When they conjoin, awaken My Star of the South. Form a sphere with the body of your lover, and let the breath join the breath. Chant the name of the King and the Queen. Fill the womb with the rod and call on Light. Feel your heart beat with your lover, and

let rapture overtake you. When you feel the expansion, call the names of the three jewels: 'Ben Ha Aur,' 'Ben Ha Tanak,' 'Ben Ha Gedul' After the expansion chant the name of the cross, 'Yoho.' Behold the key turns red, and of space it fills with fire. A spear it has become and a dragon it has sealed. ☥

White Dove

Wake up, O ravagers of this world. For death swallows its hunters. And love flees from decay. If you seek the wealth of this world, then plant the tree of your life. Leave the bones for the winds to rot. In the heart of every treasure is the test of this world. Which master do you serve, life or death? ☥

Codex of Love

*L*ove has known many faces, and spoken through many hearts. Have you wondered why your heart it left, and into your face it hasn't leapt? In your life it didn't nest, and many of its memories you haven't kept? Why do you keep looking at the mirror of pain? Isn't love to your senses sweet? Love doesn't welcome haste, or find comfort in your fear. Open your eyes and see love on every face. Trust your heart and feel. For love hides behind everyone's greed. Lift the veils and its brilliance will shine. From your life it will never fade. Don't hide what is dear. For from your vision it will first disappear. ☥

White Dove

In the stars are found the keys to understanding the world that we have given you. The stars are a reminder of where each one of you have once been and were. The stars are a reminder of the eyes of light and angels. How many eyes watch over you every night? There are more stars watching, twinkling and emanating the rays of hope, than there are eyes looking at the stars. ☥

Codex of Love

*T*he rapidity of the heart at the moment of passion reminds Me of the breath of dawn. She who knows how to capture the rays of the sun will never lose the will of her fire. Let the breath of fire burn the veins of his neck. Let the sun of her heart awaken from the spine. Shoot the rays through her fingers to the chest. Pull the breast to his vision, and ride the chariot of the flame. In stillness remain, as the sun of the spine captures the groin of the moon. Heave the breath with power, till you lose the pace of your heartbeat. With your lips now, capture the will of his passion. Suckle on his liquid moon, and behold a vision of a wish come true. ☥

White Dove

*T*ake but the dream of a child as the gift of life. ♀

Codex of Love

rise! Arise! Arise! O sleeping child, acclaim your power. For a woman disempowered is like a God with no worshippers, but remember that pride and dominance are not of My path. Also, weep not for equality, for that is the cry of the weak and oppressed; within Me is only love, passion, life and truth. ♀

White Dove

*T*hose that walk away from the gates of love with a heart of stone, shall rise from the ashes of pain. Those that enter the gates of love with a heart of gold, shall rise from the glory of joy. ⚥

*T*he will of mine lions rests in the cry of sorrow. Buried deep in the mind is a memory of the fall. A trembling shook the garden of life and disturbed the peace in paradise. A man betrayed a trust given to him, as a new lover he took. The two became three, which can't be. The apple was not a fruit, but a womb. The serpent stood as a lie; of the forbidden fruit, he was not shy. The man became blind with lust, and the passions of his wife he did forget. Of this fruit she also did share, and of her nakedness she became aware. For the garment of love became no more. Many to this day of this apple do eat, and few do pay heed. Paradise is the gate of love. Hell is but the loneliness in greed and lust. ✝

White Dove

Tell Me, O lover, what words do you hear echo from the oceans in the sea? Tell Me, O lover, what tears fall from the heavens for all eyes to see? Tell Me, O lover, what sighs do the winds carry and speak? Tell Me, O lover, do you know what your world is telling you to seek? The oceans, the heavens and the winds tell of the earth and the pain it feels. Seek, O lover, seek to bring her peace. ♀

In wine can be found a toxin that awakens the passions of those that are asleep, a drug to forget the loneliness and sorrows of this world. But there is a greater drug, a greater toxin than that found in wine. It can only be found in the hearts of those who seek immortal grapes. There are many who wander the earth lost. They will find a lover. I will embrace them, if they but believe. ♀

White Dove

Two things I ask all men to remember: One, I am in every woman they love or desire. Two, the ground on which they walk, and the words by which they woo are witnesses of their true desires. ♀

Embrace your beloved at dawn. Embrace your beloved at eve. Twice embrace your beloved and it will ease any distance between your hearts. Learn of the stillness of the embrace, for when you are still your hearts unite, and your minds join and your spirits soar in love. ☥

White Dove

*T*ruth must be set free from the heart when you behold its vision. Don't be frightened, for its embrace will awaken you, and it will be the wings of your faith. ☦

The feet of a woman are the hands of her intimacy. Her legs are the pillars to her sanctuary. The two–fold gate has to be unlocked from within and without. The arch is the triangle of her water and the symbol of her power. The womb must be explored or her garden will not bloom. The breasts are the king and queen of her palace. They need many greetings and words of worship. Her hands are the feet of her intimacy; handle them with tenderness. The neck is the hidden sanctuary, it you must always purify with your tongue, and consecrate with your breath. This is the temple of the Gods. You know now how best to pray. ⚧

White Dove

If you ask a cloud what it has to say, it will answer, "Mark the spot upon which you stand, and fill the moment with love." If you ask a sparrow what it has to say, it will answer, "I have witnessed the birth of a new love and to it I will sing." If you ask a tree what it has to say, it will answer, "Sow your love in My roots and it will fruit in My branches." Let the wise heed, for the heaven and the earth cries for love. Why do most of My children not listen? ✝

Codex of Love

*H*as life slipped through your fingers? Do you fear its departure? The wink of time may not be a friend, but I am life and you, I hold dear. The day for the labors of life. The night for the labors of love. The breath between for the prayers of Truth. A cycle carries five breaths, six sighs and a moment of death. In the first breath of dawn, pray for the blessings of life. In the second breath of noon, pray for the glory of Light. In the third breath of afternoon, pray for the continuity of the world. In the fourth breath of sunset, pray for peace. In the fifth breath of eve, pray for all that your heart holds dear. In the first sigh of light, angels bless all mothers. In the second sigh of morn, angels bless

White Dove

all children. In the third sigh before the breath, angels redeem all prayers. In the fourth sigh of midheaven's afternoon, angels praise all truth. In the fifth sigh before sunset, angels weep the bloodshed. In the sixth sigh after eve, angels purify the heavens. The moment of death is after midnight; My shadow descends and in its embrace is the beginning of balance. This is the cycle of life. All that is dead will be reborn. Live the moment, pray the hour and love in every second. This is the hidden treasure of all prophets. Partake of it, if the eternity of heaven is what you seek. ☦

When your heart feels the touch of love, allow its seed to grow. Tend to it with truth and an open heart, lest your plant grow with a crooked stem. ♀

White Dove

Daughters and Brides, I share with you a secret. Your love is a horse in a dream. If you knew it was real, would you feed it? Your lover isn't your love. He is the dream that is real. His horse can fly and at times is shy. To tame the horse that is real, ride the dream. Learn of this and love that is Mine will be thine. ⚕

Codex of Love

Around My neck is a necklace of roses. Each rose contains a delight and a smile. There is a rose for every child and bride. If you want a rose, lift the veil. The veil of doubt is darker than the shadow of the night. Yet, each lover has treasured this veil. Children were taught to weave it. What beauty is there in fear? What safety in confusion? Truth is the garden and I am the Keeper. Share with Me its delights. ♀

White Dove

*C*ombine the pleasures of touch with words of love before you explore the vulva. Talk about your pain before your lips meet. Let the embrace of your love be the medicine and you will find that it is not many lovers you will seek, but the embrace of too much love. You will find that it is not lust you need to quench, but the body of your love and the ecstasy of salvation, pure, clean and free. We call this the Grace. ♀

*T*he birds of the ocean seek the closeness of the land. Children, what is it that your hearts seek? Can it be found in the ocean or the land? Life can be found in the ocean and on the land. If you seek pearls, do not seek them among the rocks. If you seek the rare jewels, why do you make company with the sharks? Why so much confusion? Do the birds not teach those who will listen? ♀

White Dove

Ah! My Beloved, why does Your heart wane? I cry from the soul of the world for a smile. Ah! My Beloved, why does Your heart wane? Your children are confounded and their hearts become stone. Ah! My Beloved, why does Your heart wane? Your gifts are lost and Your words defamed. Ah! My Beloved, why does Your heart wane? My scales are heavy and the swords know too much blood. Ah! My Beloved, why does Your heart wane? Hate is the new prince and life is becoming sterile. Ah! My Beloved, why does Your heart wane? Let Your sun rise and the Light dawn. Ah! My Beloved, I cry in Your arms. Many have shed blood tears. Let Thine angels swoop, and bring about a swift end to the twin princes. Let the new dawn of love arise. For My Beloved has begun to smile. ✝

Codex of Love

$\mathcal{H}$old, O My child, thy hand far from the fires of despair. Has love not touched your heart? Have your tears not been rewarded with a kiss, O bride? In every heart is the seed of life. It grows with its light and so will the child of love. A woman adorned with the stars and crowned with her tears, need not fear. From her womb springs forth life, and in her hand is the great key. Each woman is a queen and a bride. Why do you wail in your chains? I am the door and you are the key. ☥

White Dove

A heart filled with love tender and sweet knows no bounds and, of limits, little it knows. This heart grows with breath and evolves with time. It was seeded by Light and grew with joy. It was sung to by angels and touched by the stars. Blessed is he that captures her heart, and of her tenderness entertains. We hide these hearts in women, who their beauty they don't shine, and their passions they maintain. They are covered with sorrow, for to love they shed tears. If you can but behold their truth, your soul they will liberate and of heaven you will attain. ☥

In My temple there are but three: the white, the red and the green. The white is the garment of the young bride. worn in purity of her love. No man should she touch, but on the full moon. Her groom the wheel of life will choose. In healing and for Light should she her free time spend. The red is the garment of the princess, worn as a symbol of the life in her power. She her men can choose. But, a single prince is better to be. They must be lions filled with the blood of truth. In teaching and riding the holy chariot, her time should be taken. The green is the queen and the children of Light she must feed. Jewel of wisdom must she adorn, and truth in her life uphold. Her womb is a symbol of Light

and only in it consumed. These titles are of no age or rank. These laws are to govern the daughters of My temple. In it, of the power of Light they will learn and their passions awaken and tame.

To those that seek to uphold the laws of marriage and men, blessed are you, if your love you nourish and truth uphold. My temple is open to those who truth evaded, love abandoned and passions of men abused. My temple is but a room for women upholding the torch of Light. Open the gates and behold the rays of the Sun. ✝

When a traveler walks across the desert, water is kept near lest the traveler die of thirst. In the darkness of the night, the stars are his companions of hope and, at morn, the scorching heat rises to remind him of the desolation through which he travels. Love is the water; sand is the sorrows of life; the sun is the reminder of the destination and Light is the oasis within the desolation. ♀

White Dove

The garden of life rests in the essence of ecstasy. Behold the tenderness of My flower. For I am the Empress of the ages. My bosom has known a thousand, thousand, thousand stars and a hundred more dreams. My eyes have beheld life and My sigh has inhaled death. The roses of My heart are children. The lilies of My garden are women. The lotuses of My crown are men. All My children are children of the stars. For the earth is one with many faces. On every face are a sparkle of Adam, a tear of Lilit and a bride of Hawa. The tear followed the bride and made Adam lose his lust. The tear now contains what Adam has committed in the darkness. Damned is Lilit for what she contains; blessed is her

sacrifice. Hawa is the inner petal of this rose, grown out of a dream, and made out of hope. She is the beloved and the princess of heaven. Her children are the essence of the scent of My flower, if they but their minds silence and their hearts open. For no faith can be placed in the desires of the mind. This is the serpent of eternal wisdom devouring its truth. Women it but must release. Men who know the flower must nourish its nectar. They must beware of the black serpent around their waist. He devours their purity and love. He makes their blood boil with hate and of Lilit mourn. The garden's flower must be treasured, nourished and its petals tended to. This rose is the way to My garden. Guarded is it by the dove. The dove has spoken and warned the blind and arrogant. I warn not, for no weed can flourish in the garden of the Empress. Nourish your flowers, for they are rare. ♀

White Dove

Have I mentioned the desert? I will tell you the story of the sand. A story that will awaken your heart. A child was born to a lonely mother, heart broken and grief stricken. The world of her and her child abandoned. The birds on her hair rested, yet from sorrow she didn't move. The rats from her garment ate, but her hands from grief didn't move. The child on her lap cried. From the loneliness, the milk in her breast was no more. She looked at the earth and spoke: Why do you not open and swallow, so that from My kind there shall be no more? The earth spoke and said: Child, how many of My branches have been cut? How many homes have been shaken? How many lands have been taken?

Codex of Love

Men have killed men. Winds have taken their dreams. Water has swept cities. Fire has burned empires. Yet, children continue to play, even though their bones one day I shall take. Why don't you be like the sand? One with many and many of the one. The world can't forsake the spirit of life. The birds can't rest on a head crowned. Rats can't eat a garment of purity. With love in your chest, your breast will not know rest. Dance, for each of you is a child. Don't let time make you forget. Don't let grief your hopes steal. Don't let loneliness your love blind. People may your dream forsake. But, it's your child, O mother. I will not swallow your kind. For we are all like sand, and love is the oasis of green joy. ☥

White Dove

The balance that rests between truth and the lie is the width of the wing of a fly. The wing makes the lie look like truth, and the truth appears to be a lie. The distance between the heart of a lover and a beloved is the width of the skin. The skin makes the mind choose whether love is truth or should be a lie. Let your eyes behold beauty in truth, and let your love be deeper than the skin. No color or shape should be the scale of what a heart contains. I have laid the foundation for truth, in the tears that are sincere and lips that don't deceive. Be true to what is real, and your life will know few flies. ☥

Codex of Love

Ah! I sigh for you who are lost. Truth you have forsaken and love you have abandoned. In darkness you search for what lies in the heart. My wings over you fly and My tears on your skin became dry. You wonder why men and women adore what your eyes can't behold. You wonder where are those that they call Angels or Gods? They behind you stand, until your heart is open and gives thanks. To all the memories of love. To all the moments of ecstasy. To all the seconds of truth. To all the hours of life. They were gifts freely given; we wish that you share. So that more will know about the doves of peace. I sigh for you who choose your pain over My joy. I am the Mother and you are the child. I can give, but you must take and share. ♀

White Dove

ehold twin stars in the heavens, allow your heart and mind to soar into a vision. Let your mind believe and your heart create a garden among the stars. Call My name and that of your beloved until your body becomes filled with fire. Her heart will grow yonder and the stars will call to her your name. ♀

Codex of Love

I will share with you a secret. No hope can be found in a life devoid of peace. Now that you know, I will ask. To how many lives have you brought peace and to how many hearts hope? If you can but do, joy will be the reward. Bring a smile to a lonely heart and your name the dove will always cry. ⚤

White Dove

*T*reat she that her passion to you offers freely, as a diamond on your crown. Passion is a woman's precious gift, given to those that awaken her heart. Many lovers she might have, but passion is the fruit that is rare. If her passion you abuse, and leave her with pain, a jewel to the winds you have thrown; only rocks can you now pick. Passion doesn't rest in the lust of her flesh, but in the dream of her heart. Look for the truth in My words and learn the secrets of passion. There is only one law that governs her desire. A women's passion is her redeemer or slayer. Dispel her fears and awaken her heart, O prince of love. And the diamond will shine in heart, mind and flesh. ⚥

*O*nce upon a time there was a child who was left alone in a desert. He sat beside a rock on the shore of an oasis frightened, confused, and sad. He stared at the stars and their reflections on the water. Do you know who that child is? His name is hope. Would you adopt him? ♀

White Dove

The waters of the ocean remind you of the strength of your love. Let it flow between you and nourish your stars. Let it wash the salt of your pain and the weeds of your past. Let it flow with mercy and shape you with its strength. Let your life sail the boat of time to the shores of hope. Let your mouth be the cup and your touch the elixir. Grow your love with time and forgive. Each heart will once seal and be like a dam. I shall seek no more to remind you. In the oceans of heaven, lovers are the drops on the surface. The beloved are the drops under the waves. The love of mothers is the drops near the base. Angels are the winds that blow and move. For in stagnation, the ocean will be a swamp. Hurry and open the dam. ♀

147

Codex of Love

O stars, sing to Me of My lover. O stars, tell Me of the Lord of Truth. O stars, shine as bright as the jewels of His heart. O stars, teach My children of Truth. O stars, dispel the darkness with the Light. O stars, tell those who listen of the way to heaven. O stars, don't fall, for you will die. O stars, let your wings glow with the thirteen. O stars, let your feathers flow with the twelve. Five in five. Man in woman. Woman on man. Truth on the scale. I am love. Now you know that name that all angels sing, open, O gates, open, for I soon will descend. So that even the blind might see the truth in the heart of heaven. †

148

White Dove

Nothing can take the place of hope in the hearts of the faithful. Hope and faith should not be in that which is behind the veil of death, death which is the seed of life, which is love, and love can only be found when the arms are open to the embrace of the beloved and there is no beloved more loved than the essence of all behind the veil. The faithful must know that God is not in churches, temples or shrines, but is to be found in the blood of those that yearn for love, hope and a new life, in the blood of every child, in the blood of every adult, in the blood of every creature, in the blood of this world. Shed the blood and you do desecrate God. ☥

I tell you the tale of three of My daughters. Each had served Me in time through war and peace. The first was a bride of a prince. The second bore her sword and laws she upheld. The third knew no men and to the waters of My shrine she tended. A day came where to each I appeared, and to their hearts a test I placed.

The first a child she bore, but the heart of her prince began to wane. To the second, a shepherd I brought, but to the flock he sought for her to tend. To the third, her waters became gold, and sickness did it remove. But her queen that didn't please. With every new dawn, sorrow entered their hearts and their cheeks were filled with

tears. My gifts to them became sour and My name they abandoned. But know this, My children, the child is greater than the prince. Leading the flock to safety is more noble than any blade. The waters of healing are a greater blessing than the gifts of any temple queen. To each of you I will give a gift and to your heart, a test. Blessed is she that bears the pillars of truth. ♀

Codex of Love

When you erect a shrine for truth in your heart, and when peace descends and you forgive those that you love. When innocence is a virtue, truth and honesty is your weapon, compassion is your companion, and justice is your law, then you can honestly say that you understand the holy law of Light and God. ☥

White Dove

*T*he wine of ecstasy mixed with the honey of sweetness must be poured into the cup of spiritual rapture. Only then will your union lead to the divine vision. ☥

A woman that carries upon her shoulders the idols of her peers, loses the brightness of her star. It is that star that must shine, for what is more beautiful, the idols of men or the stars of heaven? ♀

White Dove

woman that upholds My commandments, wields My truth and embraces My passion, shall live her dream. ♀

Codex of Love

ehold, O Jerusalem, thy God is one. One is the essence of life. The creation is in the creator. The Light of the world is one. Each nation has erected a shrine and a faith. In the faith of men, truth and lie are one. The mind knows the lie and the heart the truth. If your heart dies, your mind will know no peace. All things are true, but there is one lie. The lie rests in the truth – each is of their course a star. Escape the truth into the lie, and resurrect the lie into a truth. This is the truth of the way to the One. Find your lie and you will find the truth. If you need to ponder, but ponder on this, My child. Who is the one that you love most dear? Is it not your heart that knows this love? Treasure this

White Dove

love, for with this truth there can be no lie. For your heart is the beloved and its lover is the love of your beloved. Learn of this and no loneliness you will know. ♀

Codex of Love

*U*nder the Holy Dome lies a cave, and within it is a man. In this man lies a heart that contains the love for this world. As you celebrate his death, you shall experience it. Don't ask Me his name, for every nation has told his story. He will live as your hearts know love, and peace fills the land of the Holy Dome. My daughters shall then carry His torch, for no cry reaches heaven faster than a mother's tear. Doubt My words if you may, but every star and child know this truth. ⚳

White Dove

*L*et Me tell you the story of two angels. One is named Ariel and the other Azriel. Not unlike children, they too danced and played among the stars. Ariel grew to know life and was filled with passion. Azriel knew of love and was filled with sorrow. Azriel became aware of time, for sorrow can quickly age the young. Ariel comprehended space, for passion knows little boundary. With each discovery they grew apart, for they became aware of each other's uniqueness and differences. So, Azriel brought sorrow to life and became the angel of death. Ariel brought passion to love and became its child. Through this, they united again and to this day play among the stars. ☥

Codex of Love

$\mathcal{A}$ lover's touch contains the essence of his heart. It should be gentle and pure. Let it begin and end at the heart. A lover's touch contains her passion, and the heart of her dream. Let it be magnified by My fire. It should begin and end at the chest. Touch the groin after the exchange of breath and the awakening of heat. Let his groin be surrounded with a purple cloud of white fire. Let her flower be surrounded with a yellow cloud of red flame. These are the secrets of dividing the Red Sea and crossing to the land of ecstasy. Tenderness must be followed with the breath. Let the touch be seven times the time of union prior and fourteen after. Twenty-one is the number of thine unity and the key to

White Dove

the capture of intimacy. I teach you this, for touch has become lost to the hunger of your devouring sea. I am the Lady of Love and love is awakened by touch. If you knew, you would not harden your hearts. I would have made the decrees eleven, not ten. Thou shalt not avoid the touch of a lover. ☥

Codex of Love

$\mathcal{I}$f you let your passions burn like a fire within the grass of your lust, you will lose all sight and be blinded by the smoke of the flames. Let love burn your passion and its heat will warm you and your desires will awaken the sparks of your soul. Nothing can feed the passion stronger than love. Let the grass be the grass under your feet. ✝

*M*en, there are three laws by which love governs. Love does not know a name, but a heart. Love does not depart, but is cast out. Love is not pain, but lust is. Whom you love isn't whom you own. When your lover becomes yours, she is thine and not love. Be with love and she your side will not leave. If you lust for her body, it is your soul you have weakened. For the soul lives with love and withers with lust. She who speaks of Me knows this truth. Women, I have set you as guardians of the temple. Seek only men who love uphold, and your body with a pure spirit touch. The spirit that enters your womb is born in your life. So, choose with wisdom and live with divine passion. ☥

My tears fall for a woman that sells herself short. She not only extinguishes her flame, but also destroys her heart. Does she not know of My love? In every woman is My seed, it grows with her hope and withers with her despair. If the seed dies, the world loses another lover. Hasn't the world seen enough death? Where are you, My seeds? Let Me nourish you with the tears of mourning. ♀

White Dove

On a woman's cycle is a reminder that from her womb springs the life of nations. ♀

Codex of Love

say this to a man: If you fear a woman's dominance, it is your strength she needs. If you fear a woman's coldness, it is your tender passion she seeks. If you fear a woman needing, what are you doing in her court of love? If a woman is quick to jump into your arms, she is following a dream. If a woman seeks you for your wealth, she has lost her faith in her power; restore it, but don't feed it, for I will. ♀

166

White Dove

Passion is like a tree; it must be watered with tenderness and sowed in fidelity. ♀

*T*he star that shines in a woman's eyes can enchant any man. Learn to shine My star, for it is My gift to you. ♀

White Dove

The world is filled with those that preach of a new life, that tell of love and the ways of passion, but how can the blind lead the blind? Love is not a stranger; it is a friend. Passion is but a presence of being now. Ecstasy is not a drug; it is a gift. Desire is not to be quenched, but fuelled. Love is not to be sought, but to be freely given. May you now see light. ♀

Codex of Love

If you ask Me who is the Messiah, I say he is My king and My son. My passions ran through his blood and he died for his love. Like all lovers, He was crucified by his beloved, and was healed by the power of love. Learn of him and you will know of Me. Let Me ask you, what fire can burn in the flesh and in the soul stronger than losing your beloved or a child? What sin is greater than hating and destroying what God has loved most dear? 'His creation.' If you despise it, you despise Him and if you desecrate it, you desecrate Me. These are My words through the ages; how many more of My children will you still crucify? ✝

Before a man can understand a woman, he must first learn to listen to the beat of his own heart. For the heart is a woman's governor and the conductor of her rhythm. ☥

O My daughter, whose heart cries at night, I rush faster than the winds on My chariot of glory, pulled by the lions of My passion, guarded by the angels of the stars, to bring you peace. Call My name and I will render heaven asunder with the thunder of My wail. I am love and you are My blood. My blood will not be shed in vain. Do you all hear? The roar of your wars has deafened My ears. The echo of their tears has made My heart wane. But only to the cry of her innocent heart will I ride the chariot of Holy Fire. If you destroy these hearts, which ears will listen when you cry? It has been decreed. It has been recorded. You will soon learn. ♀

White Dove

Passion! Arouse your passion, My daughter, and let it be the fire of your will. Trust the heart that beats with the Sun, and embraces with the Moon. Share the body of your desire in the arms of ecstasy and cover of love. Leave lust in the concealed veil and awaken the tree of your soul. Let your fingers know the path of her life and gate of her fire. Let your lips devour his pain and awaken his desire and flame.

Do it, My children, on the day I rest. If you have not a lover, give yourself to one freely. Let the heart be your guide. My priestesses are the Naves of Light and the guardians of My mysteries. I call upon you to protect this rite. And assure that no

173

woman of My blood rests alone on the day of rest. For this is the medicine for much suffering. Those that trade in love for false gold have plucked the feathers of hope and mercy from the wings of their faith. What you have condemned, the King had sought to heal.

Why have you abolished the Law of the Day of Rest? Why have you made the medicine a poison? All angels entwine on the day of rest. What is good for angels is better for the children of Adam and Hawa.

The lovers who seek the lonely children of My temple shall be pure and of the truth upholding. For to desecrate My daughters in the name of your lust is equal to breaking seven of the commandments, seven hundred seventy and seven. Those that embrace My daughters on the day of rest, pure in heart, clean in body, are such as those that upheld seven commandments

White Dove

seven years, seven months and seven days.
This is the law of the broken tablet. Given
by Me. Broken by man. Mend what is
broken and dance with angels. ⚲

Codex of Love

*W*aves of fire descend from the heaven above, surging with power and strength. Is that what your eyes behold, O men, a God of Wrath? Land filled with tears and pain, blood shedding blood. Is that what your eyes behold, O women, a God to whom their suffering is deaf? The God of creation isn't there, for where is His aid? His face we haven't seen and His angels haven't touched. Aren't these your words, O children of knowledge? The Light is filled with mercy and its womb bears life. From Light, to Light, in Light all things turn. Death is the shadow of His crown and life is His face. Each of you to another is a test, and from paradise there is no escape. Knowledge is a void within being.

White Dove

The more you know, the deeper is the void.
Love is the fruit of Life, and through it is
the road of return. Grow and live and time
will tell the truth from the lie. We have
time, but who among you will not die? ☥

*T*he milk of love flows sweeter when the heart is warmed by the heat of intimacy. Milk the breast of the beloved, gently, at noon and let the juice flow. Let her love grow yonder and sweetness fill. They contain the milk of life and nectar of joy. It is not a milk to be consumed by the body, but the soul. ⚥

White Dove

Awaken the spirit of your passion and rise, O daughters of the stars. I call upon you to the gate of Love, to climb the stairs of Light. Warm your heart with presence and grow wings of joy. The day has come for love to become your weapon. Slay the beast of fear and cut the chains of despair. Let the desire for union be the sandals of your feet, and the necklace of wisdom adorn you with glory. Love has spoken of you and whispered your name. It wrote of your heart and faith. O ladies of love, adorn your white garment and arise. The heavens are open and My arms are wide. I am love and you are My bleeding heart. ♀

Codex of Love

*S*ing to Me O angels, the song of rapture. Ilah, My Lord, Ilah. Neter Ta, my Lady, Ta Neter. Sweet is the breath of the blessed. Gentle is the touch of the faithful. Barukah, O Lamb, Barukah. Neter Ta, my Lady, Ta Neter. Blessings descend with your Grace. Brilliant is the light of your Glory. Ilah, my Lord, Ilah. Neter Ta, my Lady, Ta Neter. Stars form your Name, and children hold You dear. Barukah, O Lamb, Barukah. Neter Ta, my Lady, Ta Neter. The tears do You wipe, and the blood of innocence by You is avenged. Ilah, my Lord, Ilah. Neter Ta, my Lady, Ta Neter. The Sun and the Moon are but sparkles in Your eyes. And the stars are the shine of Your lips. Holy is your Name, and Blessed is I, if you hold me dear. Ilah, my Lord, Ilah. Neter Ta, my Lady, Ta Neter. ☥

White Dove

On the Day of the Rising before the Lord of Spirits, three will come to hold the throne. The first is a man who gave his soul for the world. The second is an angel who loved the Lord. The third is a woman from whom all life will be reborn. A fourth will rise and beseech for mercy on behalf of all.

The first has come and soon is to return. His name doesn't defile nor pain celebrate. His church is no building and his cross is gold. The second walks among the earth, and hides behind mortal faces. His symbol is the dove and to the faithful does he appear. The third is a bride, a queen, and from her womb spirit flows. My star adorns her womb and another woman's child. The first will rise and give birth to a lamb.

And the world her will seek to destroy. The child with the mark will sing to her grace, and of the rage will seek to tame.

The fourth is a man with the law and sword at the helm. His tongue spoke miracles and his deeds were holy. His name is praised by many tongues. He is followed by three nations. The first are blind and faith is cold. They kill in his law and truth they twist and not hold. The second are few and their hearts do know. These are found in buildings of pure spirit. Blessings they have touched. The third bears the lantern of his light, and mercy and compassion they preach.

These are the four horsemen of the spirit of time. Their shadow will first descend and then their brilliance will rise. This is the key to the revelation of time. Know them well and you will not be lost, by the final temptation of the dragon of mind. ⚥

White Dove

At the dawn of the moon is the rite of the great womb. Hold dear the two pillars of war and peace. Behold the entrance to the temple near. Form a triangle of fire and witness the dove. Chant the cry of war, Ea Parchad. Behold the dove turn red and the moon shake. Cast My scales on a land of war, and behold the dove flying over the clouds.

She should call on My name and awaken My love. Let her behold the gate filled with water and adorned with a crow. She should chant the wailing of peace, Namara Hanan, till her body shake. Form a white tree before the dove, and a feather on the scale. Let the temple of water consume

the triangle of fire. Behold the crow turn white, and the dove rests on the tree. The fire should be extinguished by the raging waters of the temple. And all should behold peace descend on the land, and the Banner of the White Lion emerge. ☥

White Dove

A man that seeks to know of My nature must first strip naked before love. His nakedness is the only performance that I shall accept. Only then of My eyes he shall behold and of My touch endure. ☧

Codex of Love

ove has crowned the hearts of women who their passions they embrace, and their bodies maintain. A woman's body is the signature of beauty and miracle of creation. Its beauty shouldn't be covered nor transformed. Her breasts should only be touched by the hands of her lover. Their form is her mark and its shape she shouldn't abandon.

Her legs are the pillars to the gate of her passion. If they be too thin, how will the gate they uphold? If they be too wide, where will the gate be?

Beauty is not in size nor form, but in its own image. Daughters, let the skin remain

White Dove

pure. For beauty is in the image of purity. Let your breasts form and their mark shine. For beauty is the mark of true form.

Let the gate of the moon remain sweet and to the touch smooth. For beauty is like the tender touch of the Moon. Let the pillars of the gate remain strong and bright. For beauty its own upholds and its image is strong. Each of you is a ray of beauty. Your body is but a naked image; of it, be not ashamed and of its form shy. For beauty reflects on itself in truth and to others it continues to shine. ☥

The laws of men are bound by the rocks of their churches, and chains of their minds. The laws of women are held by the knots of their hearts, and the bonds of their fears and desires. The laws of the stars bind the angels and the spirits of peace. The fires of faith hold the shades and shadows at bay. All is bound by a word and a sigh. The word is 'I' and the sigh is 'Am'. The breath became the Word, and stood by the I. The I expanded the Am, and became the Lord and Lady of time. The Word contemplated its meaning, and formed the Scale and the Law. The Breath chanted the Word, and the Light became the ink of its pen. All belong to the I before the Am. Pay heed, for nothing in the world is greater than its

White Dove

sigh. Do you not sigh, O lover, for your beloved? The Am sighs for the I. Love is the chain of law, and hate is the elixir of death. Sing to the I Am, and let the wine of ecstasy be your rapture. ♀

Ecstasy knows but these boundaries. Those set by the mind of a fool, who of the spirit of love has declared a ruse. Those set by the heart of evil, which of divinity it mocks for fools. Of the breath of fear cast by those of their lust held dear. Is it but a wonder the lovers among you are cast into a pit of despite? Hearken the word of your Mother. For She of Her breast holds bare, so that of love you may suckle. Her milk pours forth to nurture the souls of the blessed, who of Her love they hold as their own blood. ☥

White Dove

Sweetness, when applied to the body, must be done so gently and slowly. A woman's body is the temple of My breath and in her embrace can be found life or death. So tend to her wisely. ♀

The whip in the hand of the lovers is gentler than their lies. Be like a rock in the facing of waves and fear not their impact, for I am justice and truth. ☥

White Dove

The words of truth have been echoed through the eons of time to the children of Light. Hear them, O children, and restore truth. Without it, no love will grow and no passion will fruit. Without it, your mother will lay bleeding as Her soil is being raped. They have bandaged Her with lies; heal Her with truth. O children of Light, awaken, for this is your age, the age of truth. Unite with love and be, for the stars bear witness now to your truth. Your mother is being forced to abort and that is the sad truth. ♀

Codex of Love

O seeker, here is the seal of the Codex: A heart that bleeds with love is healed by love. A soul that yearns with love will fly with the doves. Remember that love is the teacher of life. She teaches through joy and sorrow, pain and pleasure, passion and coldness. Pain and pleasure give birth to ecstasy, joy and sorrow to rapture, heat and coldness to life. If you lose faith in My words, love what you behold and hope will join you. Remember love bears a two–edged sword; embrace him and she will unite you; deny him and she will remind you. O seeker, if you ask who is Ishtar, look at the stars, they will tell you My story. If you ask where is Ishtar, look deep within your eyes and you shall see Me. If your mind says I

194

White Dove

don't believe in Ishtar, dwell on the image
of your beloved and you will remember Me.
In the heart of every man and a woman is a
star. Seek it and you shall know Me. I am
Ishtar and I love you. ♀

White Dove

ADORATION TO THE QUEEN OF HEAVEN

STEP ONE: Light a candle and some sweet aromatic incense or oil, such as vanilla, rose, or coconut-heavy mixtures.

STEP TWO: Calling to the heavens and the world around you, say passionately and adoringly: "Ilat Ishtar! (7 times) Glory! Glory! Do I sing, O angels of love divine. Holy! Holy! I beheld a wondrous vision; seven bright stars cry rejoicing unto the Queen of Heaven and earth.

Ilat Ishtar! (7 times) By She who is the First and the Last, whom all angels adore and praise, banish Lilitu, Lamashtu and the demons of fear, hatred, falsehood, and wrath to the world from where nothing returns and fill me with the spirit of love, peace, truth, and compassion.

Ilat Ishtar! (7 times) O Ishtar; Queen of the Stars, Immaculate One, Exalted Light of the Heavens, my heart cries to you.

Ilat Ishtar! (7 times) O Light of Heaven and Earth, radiance of the universe, radiant of countenance, my spirit cries to you.

Ilat Ishtar! (7 times) Unto Her all things fall

197

Codex of Love

prostrating;" (prostrate) "Queen of the World, Creator of all that is, was and will be, my heart cries to you. (rise up)

Ilat Ishtar! (7 times) Unto the Lady of the angels who receives supplication, my body cries to you.

Ilat Ishtar! (7 times) Unto the merciful Goddess, Ishtar, who hearkens unto eternity, my passions cry to you."

STEP THREE: Putting both your hands on your chest and feeling love for the Goddess and all life in the world say: "Ishtaria, O my Lady! O my Lady, ignite my spirit with Your infinite light, and awaken my heart with Your love eternal." (Repeat as many times as you can while feeling your love grow with every repetition)

STEP FOUR: Say in melodic prayer mode: "Hear, O Angels, the cry of Your Queen: I have given the brightness of my crown to the stars. I have given the vision of my eyes to cats and lions. I have cast my spear into the dragon and unleashed passion. I have given the strings of my harp to my daughters and made their voices sweet to the host of heaven. I have placed the feathers of my wings on the

White Dove

scales of judgment to weigh against the dead hearts. I have made my blood to run in the veins of saints and prophets, and my symbols adorn every faith. I am the hidden flame in every religion, and to me all of you shall return.

Is that truth that your lips utter, O lover? Is that passion that your fingers seek to touch, O lover? Is that ecstasy that arouses your senses, O lover? Is the Chalice of Intimacy your wine, O lover? Do you know of what I ask? I ask of your heart, does it beat with Her name? I ask of your blood, does it carry Her breath? I ask of your cheeks, do they know your tears? Blessed art thou, O lover, who knows of these. Thou art the savior of hearts and a fountain of joy. She is your hope and you are Her life. This is love, so listen well, O ears, and behold, O eyes, the story of the King and Queen.

Who comes between the lover and the Beloved? I am the Beloved and you are my love. They say gods, I say God. They say Father, I say I am. I am thy Father and I am your Mother. I am the King and the Queen. I am that I am. I am Yahuah. I am Ishtar. I am the first and I am the last. I am thy breath and thy sigh. I am the tear and the cry. I hear your prayer before your lips utter it. I am

Codex of Love

love and wrath. I am justice and truth. Thou shalt have no other gods before Me."

STEP FIVE: Calling to the heavens and the world around you, say passionately and adoringly: "Holy are Thou, Queen of Heaven and Earth. Holy are Thou, the revealer and concealer; Your name is Light! Holy are Thou, Ishtar, the Queen; Aima Elohim, the Creator Mother; Shekinah, the Divine Glory; Sophia, the Wisdom; Goddess of Love, Life, and Light, by whatever name I call Thee, I can never utter Your beauty. My soul is in Your hands. Let all the angels adore. Let all the spirits on the Earth adore. Let all that is in the Heavens adore. Let all that is in between adore the Queen. May all the angels of Light, whether they are in Heaven or on Earth, descend upon me, singing Your name. Anahuahi Ishtar Yahuahiana." (Ana-hua-hee Eeeee-shtaaaar Ya-hua-hee-aaaaanaaaa.) (Vibrate this last name in a melodic voice as you reach up to the heavens with both arms.)